The LIGHT
of OTHER
DAYS

GARY SWEENEY

THE LIGHT OF OTHER DAYS

DEDICATION

To Pop, for always being my light.

THE LIGHT OF OTHER DAYS

CONTENTS

THE LIGHT OF OTHER DAYS

ACKNOWLEDGMENTS

I would like to thank my wife, Stephanie, for her support over the course of this project. Her opinion and feedback were invaluable, as is her presence in my life. I would also like to thank my mother, grandmother, and paternal family members for sharing their memories and time to help fill in those important early details. Thank you to the curatorial staff at The Franklin Institute for their assistance with the Midvale record holdings. And last but never least, I want to thank my little girl, Audrey, for reminding me that innocence exists.

THE LIGHT OF OTHER DAYS

PREFACE

I used to imagine my own funeral in slow motion black and white, and wonder how many people would show up. I can recall staring at a wooden block of steak knives and thinking about the faces and reactions of people after they learned that I had plunged one into my own heart. I even heard the music echoing off the church walls during my funeral service. In reality, I would never have acted on any of those thoughts, but they plagued me throughout my childhood, and the more I tried to figure them out, the more I was convinced there was no reason for them. I was just a damaged person without any redeemable qualities.

The area I grew up in, Southwest Philadelphia (which we just called "Southwest"), was made up of small, sub-neighborhoods with their own separate cultures. If you ask anyone who called it home before it spiraled downhill and became crime-ridden, they would tell you it was the greatest place in the world. In my neighborhood, everyone left their front doors open, and not only anticipated but invited people to walk into their homes without knocking.

Southwest was all one massive family. At any given time, there were 50 parents sitting on their front steps, watching us play ball in the street. When I was a kid, Southwest was a safe place to be, and I wouldn't trade where I grew up for anything.

That was my public experience, however. My private experience was slightly different.

I was crippled by anxiety, depression, and introversion that forced me to spend so much time in my own head that I couldn't relate to the real world. Moreover, I was uninterested in fitting in with other people my age. Nothing about them was relatable to me; their interests were opposite mine and I wanted little to do with them. Much of my childhood was spent escaping to circumstances that were better and more fulfilling, even if they were imaginary.

For all intents and purposes, my home was fractured - not entirely broken, but fractured. If there was safety and contentment in my home, I didn't feel it. I observed everyday happenings as though they were pieces of art hanging in a gallery and I was a critic trying to interpret the meaning behind every stroke of color. If I was punished for something, my mind craved a logical explanation. I would spend hours trying to understand why something had happened and if I couldn't figure it out, it only confused me more. This led to years of analytical loops and spinning thoughts that often had no end.

My immediate family was comprised of my mother, stepfather, and great-grandparents. My maternal grandmother was still working when I was a kid, my maternal grandfather passed away when I was two years old, and my father was never in the picture (by extension, neither were his parents). While my stepfather shared the house with my mother and me, he was otherwise completely uninvolved in my upbringing aside from the occasional rebuke which seemed more like a power trip than any real interest. My mother focused most of her attention on professional advancement because she had lost a job just before Christmas 1982, leaving her with a toddler who believed in Santa Claus and no money to buy presents. The idea that one employer's decision could alter her lifestyle made her so prudent that she developed a burdening fear of walking through life without a Plan B, C, D, E, and F.

While I'll never believe it was intentional or malicious, I was left alone for many years - not physically, but emotionally. Outwardly, I never complained or said much about anything. Instead, I was nearly stoic and gave everyone the impression that nothing was amiss, and the unfortunate side effect was the misconception that I was happy. On the contrary, I was a very despondent kid, prone to bouts of unexplained melancholy and the occasional thought of suicide.

My life could have easily taken a very dangerous turn into substance abuse or criminal activity. Not only did I live in unorthodox circumstances compared to everyone I knew, but I considered myself at a disadvantage for having a genetic predisposition to bad behavior. My father's absence, as far as I was concerned, was both a deliberate choice and the result of his personality; and if I had inherited even a small percentage of that, I was doomed to echo him in the future. That thought was hammered deeper into my psyche as the years went on and he drifted further away. He was *choosing* to be out of my life, and my mother affirmed that choice by reminding me of how he had been abusive and vile, which inevitably made me hate myself more for being his child.

The only person who saved me from atrophy was my

great-grandfather. Though he went by Bruce, his full name was Wilbur Bruce Edwards; I called him Pop, and during the most formative years of my life, he was my hero.

Pop became the only constant I had, and I was fortunate to have him for 17 years. He and his wife, my great-grandmother Emily (whom I called "Gram"), essentially replaced my unbalanced household with a more traditional, loving environment.

It took me a while to decide whether or not to write this book, not because it's an unworthy story, but because there was a part of me that wasn't sure I could do it justice. It also required me to summon a part of my life that was both wonderful and horrible. Although I survived my childhood relatively in-tact, the thought of returning to Pop and Gram worried me because they're no longer here, and for a short time, I would bring them back only to leave them again.

That's the thing about memories; they allow you to drift along without reserve, to window shop through different parts of your soul, to stop and gaze, to hear music and see the refraction of light break into a beautiful spectrum of voices and old smiles. But then you have to return to actuality, and all you are left with is emptiness

When I decided to bite the bullet and write all of this out, my mind was flooded with imagery. I realized for the first time that I had somehow blocked out major portions of my adolescence, and only while wading through did some of those years rematerialize.

Each day of this project was a struggle to fit random pieces into a linear story since so much of it feels disconnected and without relevance. I walked away from it several times. I put it aside, pushed it to the bottom of my to-do list, and even considered abandoning it once or twice because I was convinced nobody would care.

Still, as I continued writing, I realized that every part of my story must mean something because nothing in our lives is unimportant; every bit of it adds up to who we become.

1. MIDVALE

I rescued him from depression.

That's what I was told.

I gave him his life back.

In April 1976, my great-grandfather on my mother's side entered a world of darkness. Three months prior, Midvale-Heppenstall, a looming giant in the Philadelphia steel industry and his employer since the 1940s, announced they were shutting down. Midvale had begun in 1867 as the Butcher Steel Works and underwent several rebrandings, first as Midvale Steel Works in 1872 (three years before landing its first contract with the U.S. Navy), then as Midvale Steel Company in 1880, and as Midvale Steel and Ordnance Company in 1915.

The company was founded to produce steel wheels for locomotives and quickly signed contracts with Baldwin Locomotive, the Pennsylvania Railroad, and John Roebling's Sons (builders of the Brooklyn Bridge). When World War I increased the need for steel, Midvale acquired three additional plants to fuel the demand (one of the shops was specifically constructed to produce eight-inch howitzers for Great Britain). The company expanded to 58 acres and began to churn out armor-piercing projectiles, high explosive shells, artillery pieces, and armor plate for the United States and its allies. After the war ended, Midvale returned to commercial products. This decreased workload resulted in the company being swallowed up by one of its largest rivals - the Bethlehem Steel Company. Bethlehem absorbed everything except for a single plant: Midvale's flagship in Nicetown, which reorganized itself as the Midvale Company in 1923. With this shift, Midvale turned its attention to armor plate steel for ships and tanks, along with propellers, shafts, and marine engines. The Great Depression forced Midvale to operate on a skeleton crew until the rumblings of a Second World War in the late 1930s reignited the military's demand for steel.

Over the next five years, Midvale entered a golden era of ordnance production for the Army and Navy. Growth continued with eight 100-ton open-hearth furnaces in operation, installation of a 14,000-ton press, and construction of an Armor Treatment Plant and the No. 9 Armor Machine Shop. Contributions to the war effort included the manufacture of six-inch armor-piercing and 14-inch high capacity projectiles for the Navy, armor plate for Navy warships, torpedo parts, turbine rotors and reduction gear forgings for warships and aircraft carriers, steel rolls for rolling airplane sheets, bearings for antiaircraft guns, submarine castings, and involvement in the Manhattan Project. As a result, Midvale was awarded the Navy E Flag with six stars denoting continued excellence. No other steel company in the nation received such a prestigious honor.

Pop was around 30 years old when he began working

in the shop midway through the war. Having spent the latter part of his 20s at the Freed Heater Company in Collegeville, PA (where he built residential products like stoves, ranges, and furnaces) he approached the job at Midvale with a sense of duty toward his country and as part of the larger effort to prevail over the Axis powers. It was practically a rite of passage for men his age to assume the patriotic responsibility of defending America by any means necessary. Though he was registered for the draft, Pop would end up contributing the brainpower of weaponry rather than the brute force of physical combat.

Finally, World War II was over and the company hit a brick wall (except for a brief reinvigoration during the Korean conflict). In December 1955, a merger with the Heppenstall Steel Company of Pittsburgh resulted in Midvale's final incarnation: the Midvale-Heppenstall Corporation.

In the years that Pop labored at the flagship plant, the scream of grinding metal would leave him exhausted, full of sweat from hours in front of an engine lathe, and aching in his legs and back. Running the machines had made it possible to support his wife and raise two daughters, but it was a grueling, thankless existence of long hours and even longer days, many of which ended with workers spilling out into the factory yard at dusk and lighting cigarettes to celebrate their freedom. As a blue-collar man with an 8th-grade education, he could scarcely hope for anything more.

But physical labor was the cornerstone of pride in those days. The men of mid-century Pennsylvania were tough and dirty with an exaggerated sense of masculinity. Their muscle was their ability to persevere, put food on their tables, and keep the house warm in the brutal northeastern winters. Overall, the postwar country was thriving economically and that meant job security was at its peak;

it also meant that the prototypical industry worker was more dedicated to his job and following the rules than finding a work/life balance. Most men defined themselves by what they accomplished. At its core, Midvale was a place of hardhats and camaraderie, of hubris, and the American dream for men like Pop, who believed that hard work would eventually lead them somewhere meaningful.

In the mornings, he would roll a pack of smokes up in his sleeve, grab a metal sandwich box, and head towards Wissahickon Avenue, an area of Philadelphia that had seen explosive industrial growth over the previous century, and which now boasted an amalgam of hard-working immigrants from diverse ethnic backgrounds such as Irish-Catholics from the famine in Ireland, and Polish-Jewish refugees from eastern Europe who were looking for factory jobs. Midvale, along with Budd Co., Nice Ball Bearing, and Philco, became part of a cultural movement that earned Philadelphia the nickname "The Workshop of the World."

Since his 30s, Pop had been working himself raw toward one goal: his pension. Putting money aside every week and getting a small investment from his employer would eventually pay off when it was time to retire, and then all of his days would be open for whatever hobby he decided to entertain in his third act. Those glorious, carefree years would be his reward for every early morning in the frigid cold, for the blistering afternoons and calloused hands, for his meticulous attention to detail, for his work ethic. As soon as he turned 62 on March 22, 1977, he would become eligible to collect on the fruits of nearly four decades.

But in January 1976, Midvale put a bullet in his heart.

The company declared that it could no longer afford the high-priced oil required to power its machinery (fuel costs tripled in 1975 and the bill was now $6 million/year), nor could it borrow an amount large enough to purchase new equipment that used *less* fuel. In addition, 900 hourly workers represented by the United Steelworkers Union (Local 8209) had been on strike since May 1975 over a contract dispute that included wages, working conditions, and benefits. Pop, along with others who were not part of the Union, were left to feel the repercussions of the strike as Midvale started to decline. The average Midvale employee was earning $3.99/hour, and one of the Union's demands was to increase pay by $3.50 over the next three years, as opposed to the $1.50 increase offered by the company. They eventually agreed on terms at the end of July 1975 (some of which were not scheduled to take effect for another two years), but the three-month strike weakened Midvale's stability.

Lost contracts and canceled orders in excess of $35 million gave the owners no choice but to look for a buyer in a last-ditch effort to save the day, but with no buyers willing to take the risk, Midvale was scheduled to close for good at the end of March 1976.

Over 600 workers were two months away from losing their only source of income. Pop was 61 years old - one year too young for his rightful pension, and too old to start over.

In their book, Work Sights: Industrial Philadelphia, 1890-1950, authors Philip Scranton and Walter Licht said of Midvale's closing:

> *The last to close of our four nineteenth-century Philadelphia plants, Midvale is soon to be demolished. For the moment, its massive forge hammers are still in place, but they will never again shake the earth with their power. Their silence leaves a bitter emptiness after a century of steel and sweat.*

It was a sudden, rapidly spreading epidemic in the steel industry. Bethlehem Steel Company, once a monster in its own right and Midvale's unintentional savior in the 1920s, had reported a net loss of over 30 percent in 1975; the Alan Wood Steel Company, based in nearby Conshohocken, lost $9.4 million in 1975 compared to a profit of $8.3 million in 1974.

Some men with whom Pop worked resolved themselves to walk away. To fight something so unavoidable was futile; with a nationwide slump in steel demand, nobody could breathe life into a bankrupt dinosaur like Midvale. Others grasped at straws, contacting city representatives to help plead with the Defense Department for salvation since Midvale had an exclusive process for making nickel alloy casings to use on the Navy's Trident submarine's nuclear reactors. Then-Mayor Frank Rizzo, himself a former crane operator at Midvale from 1940 to 1943, was considered a valuable ally who many hoped would find a solution (Rizzo had successfully helped to prevent closure in 1971), but he was unavailable for comment when it mattered the most. No help ever came; Midvale and its 109 years of history finally died on April 30, 1976.

Pop and Gram had been living on 71st & Guyer Avenue in Southwest for about 30 years. In the early years of their marriage, they moved from house to house in areas closer to where Pop spent his youth. But Gram's side of the family had lived in Southwest as far back as her great-great-grandparents in the mid-19th century, and she had far more family members around to offer support than Pop. But by the time Midvale closed, the bulk of Pop's family was dead and Gram's siblings had all married and were living their own lives. In a matter of speaking, this left them on an island by themselves.

To lie down in defeat was not part of Pop's genetic

makeup. His own father, also a machinist later in life, was a fighter by nature.

At 5'5 and barely over 140lbs, my great-great-grandfather Lawrence Edwards was known to knock out men twice his size. He was a stone-faced brawler from Paw Paw, West Virginia who could throw a punch with one hand without spilling the moonshine in the other. After moving to Pennsylvania as a young man, he joined the popular Allentown-based "Dupont's Minstrels" as a professional musician and developed a reputation for his guitar and mandolin playing, which backed a team of stellar male vocalists to a large crowd every night in Perkasie's Menlo Park around the turn of the century. But early on, Lawrence developed a drinking problem that would follow him through the rest of his life. He loved his alcohol so much that he would leave a full mason jar hidden outside whenever he visited with friends (several times throughout the visit, he would make an excuse to disappear). I always imagined him sitting against a tree at dusk, alone, with a shirt soaked through from the humidity, looking over his shoulder before each sip while fireflies danced in the surrounding fields. The truth was probably far less romantic. Family lore paints him as a hair-triggered autocrat who feared no man and had the scars to prove it.

Maybe Lawrence's perpetual drunkenness made him fearless, or maybe life had beaten all of his empathy away. Whatever the case, he would never let another man get the best of him. I can only assume that his father's example gave Pop a metric by which to judge his own fortitude. It was a stark contrast to the example set by his mother, who would send him off to school and tell him that she would "probably be dead" by the time he returned home, which caused him to shift in his desk throughout the day —

worried that he might discover her corpse later in the afternoon. Pop became someone who forced himself to survive by any means necessary, regardless of his fear or tendency towards obsessive vigilance. So, when Midvale closed its doors, he began to look for windows.

From a legal standpoint, he was not in the best position. He couldn't afford an attorney, and even if he could, the scale of Midvale's insolvency was well-documented. In effect, a successful lawsuit would ultimately fail to yield anything except for the personal satisfaction of winning. Although his pension money was deducted from earnings and invested for him by Midvale, the company was under no legal obligation to return that money to any worker under the age of 62.

Pop's first move was to contact his local committeeman, who acted as a liaison between the public and lower-rung political figures. These men were big fish in a small pond, often solicited for favors ranging from issues with parking stickers to petty neighborhood conflicts. Here, the committeeman's influence did not reach far enough; he could only direct Pop towards those with more clout - which, after a series of failed meeting attempts with various representatives, turned out to be Arlen Specter. A well-known and connected force, Specter had been Philadelphia District Attorney from 1965 to 1974 and spent years working at the law firm Dechert, Price & Rhoads (he would become a U.S. Senator in 1980). Specter's proletariat background made him approachable, and it was hoped, better equipped to advocate on behalf of the middle class. But regardless of Specter's maneuvering or any time he may have given the issue, it was another dead-end.

Though Pop struggled repeatedly to bring his problem to someone who cared, the harsh truth was that Midvale had slipped through a loophole. As stated in the specifics of its pension plan:

> *The Company by action of its Board of Directors may terminate this Plan at any time. In the event of such termination the Company shall be free to discontinue the payment of benefits theretofore granted under this Plan and to grant no further benefits, and the Company and the Members shall make no further contributions to the Fund.*

In other words, Midvale could legally discontinue benefits already funded by its contributions and deductions from Pop's earnings before the plant closed. As unsavory and immoral as it may have been, it was not against the law.

Months of pleading, letters, phone calls, and in-person meetings resulted in little more than basic sympathy. His resources exhausted and his optimism fading, Pop took odd jobs around his neighborhood - including landscaping (when manual push-mowers were the only option) - to make ends meet until he could collect Social Security.

Then in early 1977, there was a glimmer of hope.

A British entrepreneur named Ian J. Westwood-Booth vowed to purchase Midvale, modernize the plant, and rehire 1,000 workers who were unceremoniously railroaded by the shutdown. Westwood-Booth's plans were grandiose and futuristic; in his mind, the new Midvale would revolutionize steel production and bring a wave of prosperity back to the city. In February 1977, Westwood-Booth, deemed the "new owner," boasted a purchase price of $13 million and planned a settlement for mid-May. The problem, however, was that funding from the Philadelphia Industrial Development Corp (PIDC), had not been secured, and Westwood-Booth's vision depended entirely on the government's investment.

Later that month, a conflicting newspaper article reported the purchase price as $7.1 million but confirmed that Midvale would reopen on June 1 with Westwood-Booth assuming $5.9 million in pension liabilities for the displaced workers. As soon as the plant was operational, the men would be rehired over a 15-month period. Yet, the PIDC had not committed to participating, citing incomplete details and admonishing Westwood-Booth's small personal investment of $500,000. Nevertheless, the businessman remained confident and publicly stated his intent to become President of the resurrected company.

By September, the PIDC had pulled out, and Westwood-Booth was looking for alternate financing. He claimed that his plan was still alive, but blamed the PIDC for refusing to guarantee a $5.2 million loan (PIDC ultimately called the venture "high risk"). Miraculously, Westwood-Booth had secured financing agreements for most of the project's cost, which had inflated to roughly $40 million. He enlisted U.S. Rep. Robert Nix to research federal funding options, and Nix went so far as to discuss the Midvale situation with President Jimmy Carter but received no commitment from the White House.

Pop was becoming tired; the theft of his earnings and a feeling of helplessness took an emotional toll that slowly became a deep sadness. With no savings, plans for a comfortable retirement were now unrealistic.

For a man who had worked steadily and pulled his own weight since his early teens, having no regular routine was foreign terrain. There were no alarm clocks or lunchtime whistles signaling the appropriate time to unscrew his thermos of stale coffee (with a possible touch of whiskey mixed in for good measure), no uniforms, welding sparks, or benches upon which to discuss sports with other men; there was only silence.

When Pop was working and the future still looked promising, he spent the majority of his spare time in the basement. It was a concrete sanctuary of ratchets and coffee cans filled with old screws - the perfect place for a man of his precision. It was also where he crafted the small ornaments that decorated his home. He could spend hours tinkering around to the buzz of his radio while Gram sat upstairs in the kitchen, blowing smoke from a long Saratoga and watching game shows on their thirteen-inch black and white television.

The living room staircase was his pièce de résistance. It was ornate and sleek; the bottom step curved around in a half-circle and the railing followed it. The wood was lacquered and the trim looked to have been painstakingly shaped by hand. I can still hear the pride in his voice whenever he reminded me of his masterwork. "You know, Gary, I built those steps myself," he would tell me.

But all of those things were suddenly meaningless.

The house that had once been his magnum opus was closing in on him. The basement was locked in stillness for eternity, a forgotten graveyard of tools situated oddly and covered in a blanket of dust. His bright red and gold hand-painted bowls and other items lining the shelves in his living room started to fade. The cement porch out back, once a conduit for talks and summertime beers with longtime neighbors and another example of his craftsmanship, cracked from neglect. The staircase was now a way to escape. Everything that defined him and made him special no longer seemed to matter.

Regardless of his stature to the people who loved him, Pop could only measure worth in his ability to provide; and though there was no shame in the humility of working for his neighbors, he was a skilled machinist capable of building engines and munitions.

My great-grandparents' bedroom was small and unremarkable - a twin bed with a worn mattress and an old art deco vanity with a large circular mirror, permanently streaked by years of wiping it clean. A standalone wardrobe leaned against the left wall, filled with a collection of hats and dated clothing. It was all that he and Gram needed at their age, but his melancholia suddenly made the emptiness more noticeable.

Under the weight of his wife's strong perfume lingering in the air, with sunlight cutting through the room and drawing attention to scuffs on the wooden floor - in a hush broken only by the muffled sound of children playing in the street, Pop began to waste away in self-imposed exile, a broken man with repetitive thoughts.

He stayed that way for almost two years.

2. FATHERS AND SONS

I have one video of my father. It was taken during Christmas 1987 and shows him exactly as he was, or as I was told he used to be. He's wearing a plaid shirt with a sleeveless vest, and a trucker hat is covering a thick head of disheveled hair. His ever-present mustache contours perfectly as he cracks jokes and sings along with the music blaring from the nearby stereo system.

First, it was John Denver. "Country roads...take me home...to the place...I belong..."

Then, it was George Jones. "Just follow the stairway...to this lonely world of mine...."

Meanwhile, his second wife and my three half-brothers weave in and out of frame, enjoying what appears to be the all-American holiday celebration for a lower-class family: wood paneling, mismatched lamps, profanity, alcohol, and endless Marlboros. In one scene, my father plays happily with my youngest brother, laughing as he tickles his belly with a toy chainsaw; in another scene, he flashes his middle finger at the camera and awkwardly sways his body to

Marvin Gaye's *Let's Get It On*. While cursing the camera's invasiveness, he plays the stage like a thespian vying for the role that would define his career. None of it makes absolute sense; yet, in the dull colors and muddied sound, I gained a better understanding of him.

Until I obtained a copy of that tape, everything I knew about my father came from the secondhand remembrances of other people, and they were never good.

"Your father is white trash."

"Your father has a horrible temper."

"You're better off not knowing your father, he's a deadbeat."

Those statements forced me to have a low opinion of the man responsible for my existence. There was no objectivity; he was just a *bad person*. If I had been told anything good about him, I might have questioned his absence in my life. Instead, constant negative reinforcement about his character did nothing but validate his proclivity for irresponsibility. The only positive note on which everyone could agree was that he had been extremely intelligent, but chose to use his brain for avoiding the law.

To be fair, my father was a doomed person, raised by *his* father to believe that men were superior to women. He was a physically- and emotionally-abused child who grew up clenching his fists in private until he was old enough to take it out on other people. He came from a large family with several brothers and sisters, and his father used to make the boys fight each other on the lawn as a means of entertainment for him and his barroom friends. If my father or any of his siblings dared to object, they were smacked across the face. My paternal grandfather could be a monster, and his quick temper made it easy to rule by fear; his children and his wife were to be seen and not heard.

This turned my father into a bitter adult who hated authority. Everything he knew about the world was tainted by the pessimism of his upbringing. When a problem arose, it was solved by yelling or swinging; it was the only coping mechanism he had, and without much life experience, he was guaranteed to repeat the patterns he saw as a child. My father had a deep, commanding voice that sounded threatening, and that was advantageous for a man who needed control. But inside, he was still a terrified kid who never came to terms with being unvalued.

When he and my mother met, he wore a friendlier mask.

My paternal grandparents had been friends with Pop and Gram since the early 1960s. In their heyday, they were part of a crowd that met in New Jersey on Friday and Saturday nights at old haunts like The Krazy Kat and Reggies. The same people frequented these hole-in-the-wall "Country and Western bars" every weekend, and meeting up became more of a tradition than a plan. Pop and Gram, along with my father's parents and a few others, christened themselves the "Over the Hill Gang." For more than 10 years, they had a running group date.

On December 3, 1977, with the battle to save his pension still waging and Pop despondent, Gram wanted to take his mind off what everyone knew would inevitably be the end of Midvale. It was a Saturday night, and Pop and Gram were leaving for The Mustang Lounge in Almonesson, New Jersey. My mother being nineteen and bored corralled a friend and they tagged along because they planned to meet two band members with whom they were loosely acquainted; in a twist of fate, my mother and her friend were stood up and spent most of the evening complaining about how pointless the night had become. Later, my mother's friend noticed Gram dancing with a young man and pointed it out; my mother found him attractive, and Gram immediately danced him over to the table.

"Denise, this is Gary. Gary is going to ask you to dance. Right, Gary?"

It was the first time my parents had seen each other. As it happened, my father only stopped by the Mustang Lounge to visit his parents briefly and had planned to leave after a few minutes. Gram's quick-footed apprehension gave him no choice but to stay longer than anticipated, and he asked my mother to dance. Six days later, he proposed and she accepted. They married a few months later at the Cecil County Courthouse in Elkton, Maryland on April 22, 1978, and unbeknownst to them, I was in attendance.

In a less-dysfunctional setting, the rest would be history.

After learning of the pregnancy, my father was elated despite my mother's suspicions that he had sabotaged her birth control. The women in his family were known for having children in rapid succession because their husbands wanted it that way. During my mother's pregnancy, he was considerate and attentive like he was monitoring an injured squirrel in a shoebox. His first child would be a baptism by fire, his ticket into the exclusive Sweeney brotherhood where all good sons procreated without thinking of the long-term responsibilities. Most importantly, he would be a man - both in his own eyes and in his father's. He made sure that my mother never exerted herself, at least in the beginning.

By the second trimester, traces of his suppressed rage began to surface.

The summer of 1978 had been sweltering. My parents were renting a house from a family member and barely making the payments. It was a typical room with no air conditioning, and that meant any relief from the heat had to come through the windows or from the obnoxiously loud box fans that almost everyone had. My mother was sprawled across the bed, fanning herself incessantly to battle the humidity when she heard an ice cream truck rumbling down the street. My father wouldn't allow her to handle money - not because she was incapable, but because he needed to hold a position of power. Managing her own finances would give her a taste of independence and his insecurity dictated that any measure of freedom he allowed could be exploited. If she wanted money, she asked him, and whether or not it was granted depended on his mood. On good days she would witness a more nurturing side, but when he was aggravated it was almost best to say nothing. That day, it was entirely too hot to care, and she asked him for money to buy a cone.

By the time she had the dollar in hand and threw on her maternity shirt, the jingling melody was already a couple of blocks away. Four months pregnant and sweating, she bolted past curious neighbors who probably wondered why her husband hadn't offered to chase the truck on her behalf. When it finally stopped for a group of salivating kids, my mother panted heavily and waited her turn. It was another ten minutes before she made it back to the house, finishing her treat on the way. The moment she came through the door, my father launched into a verbal attack that included an accusation of infidelity. He had convinced himself that her wanting ice cream had been a clever ruse to escape for the purpose of cheating on him and that her conveniently missing cone and bedraggled appearance was somehow irrefutable proof of an affair.

My father could never hold a job for more than a few months. Shunning authority had its pitfalls, especially with a pregnant wife, bills, and a longstanding obsession with being in charge. His priorities out of sync with adulthood, he would often apologize for dramatic behavior with flowers while ignoring the fact that their utilities were days away from being cut off. Regardless of how many past-due notices were piling up, my father had a unique ability to shoot himself in the foot. He would show up to work late, get reprimanded, then tell his boss, in no uncertain terms, to go fuck himself.

During the later months of my mother's pregnancy in late 1978, my father managed to curb his temper long enough to work at the Woodbury Battery & Ignition Company. This kept him away during the day, which not only relieved her of his mood swings but gave Pop a reason to leave the house since she had doctor's appointments and he was still actively driving his 1971 *Willowmist Green* Buick Skylark.

There hadn't been any word on Midvale's resurgence since May 1978, and even then, it was no more than a brief mention in the newspaper, barely enough to let the public know that a plan was circling the drain. Pop's Social Security had begun to lighten the financial strain of daily living but his depression was unrelenting. And somewhere in this small pocket of time, he developed severe Glaucoma. Specialists from both Wills Eye Hospital and Scheie Eye Institute treated him until his case was deemed so critical that his left eye had to be removed through enucleation. This meant that the ball itself would come out, but the muscles attached to the outside to control movement and other tissues surrounding the eye within the bony socket of the skull would be left intact. By the time they scheduled the procedure, Pop was living with the equivalent of 80lbs of pressure on his eye, which his physician noted was "enough to make someone want to blow their brains out." Afterward, he was fitted with a glass replica, the blue iris nearly indistinguishable from its real counterpart.

Still, my mother was his first grandchild and secretly his favorite, so he made himself available to drive her around as soon as his eye had healed.

Throughout his life, Pop was known for committing faux pas to an extent rivaled by almost nobody. It was a personality trait that couldn't be shaken, regardless of how many times he embarrassed others around him, or how often they shushed him through gritted teeth. He simply wasn't inhibited by society's definition of tact, nor was he aware of it. There was no malice behind his forwardness, there was an innocence that suggested he was somehow above the pettiness associated with being offended, which made him talk without thinking.

When my mother needed a ride to the OB-GYN for a third-trimester checkup, Pop readily obliged and sat in the waiting room, looking to engage with one of the other ladies who were clearly preoccupied with other matters. Glancing over repeatedly at a young woman until he saw a divide in the attention she was paying to a magazine, Pop dived into one of his usual solecisms.

"Hey, you know I'm gonna be a great-grandfather?" he asked. "I bet you would *never* think that!"

"Oh, really? Wow!" the woman replied diplomatically.

"Yeah, I'm only 63 years old. But it's true. Matter fact..." Pop repositioned himself directly next to the woman and leaned his cheek further into her personal space than most people would have. "Feel my skin." He waited until she reluctantly touched his face with the back of her hand. "You ever feel skin that smooth? It's like a baby's *ass*." The woman nodded and smiled uncomfortably before pulling her hand back. Pop was oblivious to her apprehension and grinned like he had just proven some universal point about the merits of aging gracefully. Before ending the conversation, he added a final question: "So, what are you here for, hon?"

Christmas 1978 came and my father was in a jovial mood since my birth was imminent. Holiday lights were strewn across lawns and plastic candy canes lined the streets; it was practically tradition in the neighborhood to go overboard with decorations, but the ambiance it created added another layer of warmth to anyone who was happy.

As the New Year arrived, my mother agonized over the wait but felt relieved that I had not been born a week early, since her medical insurance wouldn't offer maternity benefits to any woman married less than nine months. My original due date was January 6th, but it was another two weeks before she checked into Methodist Hospital in South Philadelphia on January 19th and was given Pitocin (a synthetic version of oxytocin) to strengthen labor contractions. After wrapping a monitor around her abdomen and running some tests, the doctors sent her home. That evening, she woke up with severe pains and was rushed to the hospital. Pop and Gram stayed awake all night, pacing around the house and chain-drinking coffee as they waited for news.

My mother went into labor for 14 hours, after which tests and x-rays revealed that the space between her pelvic bones was too narrow and she needed a Caesarean section. The doctors tied her to a padded table and placed a gas mask over her face. She took a couple of breaths, felt a momentary slip into peacefulness, and lost consciousness. Later, she was shaken by a nurse and instinctively felt her stomach upon waking up, only to find the large pregnancy bump gone. "You had a nice, big boy," someone said randomly. By the time she called friends and family to share the news, she learned that Gram had already made the telephone rounds.

I was born on January 20, 1979, at 1:52 p.m. and named Gary Dale Sweeney, Jr., after my father.

Two months later, word that Midvale had finally been purchased began to spread throughout Philadelphia, though it was not the kind of purchase that the ousted workers had been seeking. The Park Corporation paid $730,000 for the facility and announced plans to renovate the space before leasing it out to other companies. Surprisingly, Westwood-Booth had thrown his name into the proceedings for a second time and was still vowing to reopen the plant despite the fact that it was financially impossible. The Philadelphia Inquirer reported that investors would have to put up a minimum of $14 million in cash on top of the federal government having to guarantee a loan of $60-$70 million. Even in the event that Midvale could operate again, it would take at least five years for the investors to see a return. Westwood-Booth was delusional at best and Pop finally stopped believing in a happy ending for his pension money.

Despite my birth bringing some joy into Pop's life, he continued to retreat further from his family. It would be another couple of years before he and I spent any real time together. The first year and a half of my life was filled with turmoil. My father was a veritable Jekyll and Hyde, making his presence unbearable when he was unjustifiably angry, and barely tolerable when he was calm. His cynicism eclipsed most opportunities for growth because good fortune made him suspicious and he would accuse whoever treated him kindly of having an ulterior motive: textbook self-loathing. Eventually his inability to work steadily forced him and my mother to abandon their rented house and move in with my maternal grandmother, which he hated. My father was only a bully in the shadows; he had no problem pushing others around as long as nobody was watching. If he became enraged in mixed company, he would smolder in private, sometimes for hours, until he could unleash the fury of Hell. But living with his mother-in-law caused him such discomfort that he avoided interaction, choosing instead to isolate in the upstairs bedroom with me and my mother. It was a prison of his own design, one he both needed and resented having to utilize.

On July 25, 1980, he snapped.

My father had acted viciously throughout the day. He was loud, sarcastic, and hostile, and attempts to reason with him were pointless. Pop was visiting and my maternal grandmother was in New Jersey with relatives. Abruptly, my father (outside of Pop's earshot) ordered my mother to take me for a walk in the stroller, which she initially refused to do because of the demand. But when he followed that up by threatening her, she took me out of the house and walked until stopping in front of St. Irenaeus Church; there, she prayed for the strength to leave him.

Upon returning home, my mother ran into a friend who wanted to show off her recently purchased car. Defiantly, my mother handed me to my father and left with her friend without asking, which for my father was an unforgivable sin. In the few minutes she was gone, my father sat alone in his mother-in-law's living room with the sound of his own wrath pin-balling back and forth.

Soon after, my mother ascended the front steps of the house. When she reached the top step, the wooden door swung open and my father reached through to grab her by the hair. After dragging her inside, he began slamming her head against the door repeatedly until she was disoriented. Despite her confusion, my mother realized that Pop had gone home while she was out so there wouldn't be anyone to save her from my father's pent-up aggression as I sat in a playpen, too little to grasp the danger of my surroundings. In the past, my father had never hesitated to throw a punch or shove my mother to assert dominance. On occasion, he would grab her head and shake it while screaming in her face. Those instances were frightening but short lived. This time, however, his anger was so intense that my mother believed he was finally capable of beating her to death.

But, in this wave of violence, there was a turning point.

My mother's abject fear had instantly become some kind of fire inside of her. Instead of cowering as soon as he stopped his assault, she punched him back. Incensed, my father chased her up to the second-floor landing, caught her, and threw her back downstairs where he kicked and punched her until she was bloodied and bruised. Swinging hastily, he had failed to consider the effects of his actions; but when he finally calmed enough to see her pummeled face, he panicked, ran upstairs, and locked himself in the bedroom.

Instinctively, my mother called her mother in New Jersey and told her to throw my father out of the house. As the homeowner, my maternal grandmother was the only person who could legally have my father removed by the police. My grandmother raced home and dialed 911; when the police arrived, they rapped their fists against the upstairs bedroom door and ordered my father to come out. "Mr. Sweeney, let's go. You have to leave. Your mother-in-law wants you out of her house," they declared several times. He finally opened the door and argued with the officers all the way down the stairs and into the living room. Then, he looked at my mother with an all-too-familiar scowl. "You're a bitch!" he screamed. By that time, my grandmother had taken me out of the playpen and put me on her lap (she later said that I was shaking); and after she yelled at my father for insulting my mother, he responded with the same insult towards her as the police escorted him outside.

Instead of taking him into custody, the officers released my father to stay with some friends of our family who lived only a few houses away. He slept on their couch that night and returned to New Jersey early in the morning. Still, the trauma of the fight caused my mother to avoid leaving the house because she assumed that my father was somewhere nearby, waiting for the opportunity to catch her alone.

Days passed before a kid from the neighborhood handed my mother a letter. My father had thrown the kid a few bucks and enlisted him as a messenger, knowing my mother would be more receptive to a child than to a man who had physically and mentally abused her for the past 18 months. He had lost the job at Woodbury Battery & Ignition Company and was working intermittently on a produce truck that sat on the corner of 70th & Grovers Avenue, walking distance from my maternal grandmother's house. The letter was a stereotypical male outpouring of explanatory rhetoric, full of apologies and promises. His remorse convinced my mother that he was less likely to be confrontational, at least initially.

Cautiously, she began visiting him off and on at the produce truck, and for a while, there was no hostility or bad behavior, but my father couldn't suppress his true character for an extended period of time. His argumentative nature soon overpowered the role he was playing and my mother stopped visiting, so he quit his job and left Philadelphia.

3. THE LOVE WE DESERVE

After my father went back to New Jersey, my mother heard that he was seeing a girl who advised him to steal me away without warning. He had threatened to steal me so many times that my mother would not allow him to visit me without her being present, and he refused that arrangement. So, they were locked in a standoff and I was in the middle. When his relationship with the new girl predictably ended, my mother began taking me to see my father's parents. My father was usually there, acting friendlier because he didn't have a stronghold anymore. Then suddenly, there were rumors that he began hitchhiking around the country with no real destination in mind. Presumably, this was his way of searching for something. He hadn't experienced a real childhood, and his shotgun marriage had failed soon after it began. For all intents and purposes, he was a nobody without prospects. My mother was no longer threatened by him and I had become unreachable because his involvement required him to contribute financially, and he couldn't. Even if it hurt him, he would have to keep his distance.

That August in 1980, Midvale was suddenly back in the news. Park Corporation's plans to divide the plant into sections had never come to fruition. Seemingly out of nowhere, Westwood-Booth stood in front of the public for a third time and declared that he had firmed up an $80 million financial package that would cover the cost of buying Midvale back. This was different than all the previous attempts; this looked like real hope. Pop was interested again. He had long abandoned the idea of returning to Midvale for work, but if the company was coming back, it was conceivable that his pension could be reinstated. The only remaining obstacle was that Midvale Co. would need a U.S. Defense Department guarantee of $43 million in loans, and as impossible as that sounded, it was being considered. But, then-Governor Dick Thornburgh, who had previously lauded the initiative to reopen Midvale, wrote a letter to Defense Secretary Harold Brown withdrawing his support.

Several political entities admonished Thornburgh for his shortsightedness, especially with the potential for 1,400 new jobs. In response, Thornburgh claimed to have based his decision on information that the revived Midvale would produce products already forged in other parts of Pennsylvania. In other words, he would not agree to use federal tax dollars to ignite a competition that could jeopardize thousands of men and women. Despite Thornburgh's objections, Westwood-Booth signed an employment contract with the United Steelworkers and promised to give initial preference to former Midvale workers. The Defense Department agreed to weigh the options and issue their decision in a short amount of time.

Four days later, they rejected the loan guarantee. Midvale's resurrection was never discussed again. Any hope Pop may have had for his pension money was gone. There would be a few scant newspaper articles on Midvale in 1982 and 1986, respectively, but they were no more than retrospectives on its place in the history of steel forging.

With my father gone I was left with Pop and Gram while my mother worked during the day. On one occasion I had been in a playpen acting restless until I figured out that I could burrow holes through the net and use them as makeshift steps to climb out. I did this several times until I was put in a different playpen with fabric that I couldn't tear; to remedy this, I jumped up and down until the bottom collapsed and then crawled out underneath. Pop took this to mean that I was unhappy being confined. He began taking me with him on short trips to the store and to the chagrin of my mother who saw me perched on a stool in my diaper as she walked by the open door on her way home from work, to the corner bar while he reminisced with friends.

In late 1980, my mother filed for divorce from my father. It was finalized on October 16, 1981, her 23rd birthday. In April of 1983, my father remarried to a woman named Bernice, who was 8 months pregnant with their son, my first half-brother, Joe. Bernice was a more submissive woman who fit perfectly into my father's world. She was easy to control and outwardly content to hitch her wagon to a falling star. While I never knew the details of my father's second family as they were happening, I eventually learned that he and Bernice ended up having three boys and stayed together, though the turbulence was evident from the beginning and would ultimately affect the infrequency of my father's presence in my life.

My mother married my father for love, and it hadn't

been enough. He didn't know how to change, and more importantly, he couldn't be introspective. Actions and behaviors considered normal on his side of the family were blatantly harmful and sometimes cruel. But, while my mother succeeded in getting away from the union and removing me from its negative influences, she still understood that her love for my father left a dent in her armor. If she was to stay diligent about raising me in a controlled environment, she couldn't allow something as unpredictable as love to interfere.

When I was four years old, my mother met Rick.

Rick was the opposite of everything my father represented. He worked a steady bank job, paid his bills on time, and had a mild demeanor. It was nearly impossible to rattle him, and that level of calm was attractive to my mother, who had been used to my father's volatile outbursts without provocation. But if Rick's consistency was a green check in the right column, his interest in me (or, for accuracy's sake, his *tolerance* of me) pushed him into a different category altogether. Though my mother had come to terms with single-parenthood long before Rick's arrival, there was suddenly an alternative, and that meant her hope for a nuclear family was alive again.

Still, I would be a stepchild, and stepchildren carried a stigma. In most cases, they were the product of poor judgment and would, therefore, become *baggage* in the eyes of future love interests. This made it difficult for any woman to find a partner willing to get involved, not only because men typically have an innate mammalian aversion to the presence of another man's children, but because the child will never exhibit the traits, behaviors, or personality of a stepparent. Furthermore, the stepparent will be expected to carry the same financial burden as a biological parent, but without garnering an equal amount of respect and while living in a house with an imbalance of authority. It's not an alluring proposition for most, but there was Rick with a smile on his face and a mountain of reassurance.

Life would be great.

The glaring issue, however, was that my mother didn't love Rick. She thought, with time, love might creep into their lives, but the real goal of the marriage, at least from her perspective, was stability for both of us.

Rick was a quirky man. I was too young to understand it then, but in retrospect, I'm convinced he suffered from Obsessive-Compulsive Disorder. He carried an umbrella with him every day, regardless of whether or not there was rain in the forecast. I also remember his method of opening and closing doors. Before he would twist the doorknob, he would hover his hand over it for 20-30 seconds. It was ritualistic and strange, but also normal because I had no real means of comparison. When I was a teenager, there were times he would let my friends and I tag along with him to the mall. If any of us dared to adjust his car seat by the slightest angle, he would know it immediately. Whenever he made himself something to eat, he would hide the plate or bowl somewhere to avoid washing it, and without fail, the various trunks and suitcases he stored in the basement - filled with baseball cards - were always locked. In some ways, he was like a grown child. It wasn't entirely troubling once I was old enough to warrant some freedom, but between the ages of 5 and 10, I was riddled with confusion.

Still, he wasn't violent, and that made him better than my father.

Rick's mother was an old Jewish woman who lived alone in the building she owned at 5th and Pine. Every so often we would pick her up and take her out to lunch on

Sundays, and she usually made sure to bring an old book from Rick's childhood with her. I always felt it was more about ridding herself of clutter than it was handing me a gift, a thought later solidified when I overheard her scolding Rick for getting involved with a single mother and raising "another man's child." That was who I became for a while - another man's child, the child of a man who was nowhere to be found unless you happened to visit New Jersey and asked the nearest police officer which jail was holding him at that particular moment. I don't know if Rick ever believed he had a part in raising me; I was just there, like an extra box that my mother forgot to donate before moving in with him. And oddly, I didn't know that he was *supposed* to be raising me; he was just...there. Somehow, we coexisted with a mutual understanding, never spoken aloud but acknowledged, that our only real connection was through my mother. One on one, however, there was nothing, and I don't think either of us cared.

Since Pop was my only male role model, I had a hard time processing the *idea* of Rick because, unlike Pop, he was closer in age to my real father, and since my father left when I was a baby, I had no experience with a man that age. Pop was like a safety net following me through life, while Rick was an authority figure forced upon me, except Rick knew nothing about being a parent and laying the ground rules for a child because he could barely manage himself.

About 10 years before meeting my mother, Rick experienced an emotional shock on the morning of September 1, 1974. His father, a Rabbi at the Kesher-Israel Synagogue at 412 Lombard Street, was shot twice and killed during a botched robbery attempt at that morning's prayer service. Rick was called by the police to identify his father's body, while his mother yelled at him from the stoop of their home to "keep his mouth shut" and to tell the police nothing. It was a strange order for a newly-widowed woman to give, but she feared retaliation if the assailant (later determined to be two men) were to find out where she lived; both killers were on the loose for months before their apprehension, and one of them was acquitted. That event triggered a detour in Rick's mind. He became someone who floated through existence without regard for most things unless it was his latest fixation. Losing his father seemed to impact his ability to fully connect with others; the result was that none of his concerns were invested in other people, and that would eventually become a harbinger of doom.

Rick's greatest passion was money. He wasn't rich by the slightest stretch, but he was hyper-focused on it. Everything he did centered on money in some way. If he was suddenly buying sports memorabilia, it was because of its potential market value, not for sentimentality reasons. He expected to inherit his mother's building after her death and anticipated his eventual windfall as though he was looking forward to retiring on an island, alone. Perhaps the most telling was his refusal to adopt me. My mother didn't want him to adopt me, but he had already objected to the idea because he was afraid my mother would leave him and then he would be trapped paying child support. But again, his financial vigilance was a great contrast to my father's indifference about bills, jobs, and general responsibility.

He and my mother eloped to Elkton, Maryland on June 5, 1984, and got married in the same courthouse as my mother and father.

About the same time that my mother eloped, Pop seemed to finally let go of the idea that he would ever see a penny from Midvale, although some of his coworkers were still battling the company. The day after my mother's marriage to Rick, on June 6, 1984, a man named Joseph Piech sued the Pension Benefit Guaranty Corporation (PBGC) on behalf of the Midvale employees whose pensions were absorbed in the company shutdown. In the lawsuit, it was divulged that Midvale had administered three separate pension plans: (1) a plan for the hourly employees (the Hourly Plan); (2) a plan for the plant guards (the Guards' Plan); and (3) a plan for the salaried employees (the Salaried Plan). Midvale filed a notice of intent with the PBGC to terminate the plans, as required by the Employee Retirement Income Security Act (ERISA). Upon determining that the plans' assets might not be sufficient to pay guaranteed benefits, the PBGC had itself appointed as trustee of the plans on April 22, 1977 and fixed their termination date of April 30, 1976.

Pop's pension would have fallen under the Hourly Plan, which provided that participants who attained sixty-two years of age and had completed fifteen years of continuous service had a vested right to pension benefits. Like Pop, Joseph Piech had been sixty-one years old at the time of Midvale's closing and had nearly forty years of service with the company as of April 30, 1976. Under the terms of the plan on that date, the PBGC determined that Piech was not entitled to any vested benefits despite his many years of service to the company. The district court upheld this decision on September 11, 1984. It was the final sputter of resolve left in the fight to recoup the lost pension money, and it failed. Pop had become so accustomed to disappointment that I imagine he would have exhaled and flipped his newspaper to the sports section for a rundown on the upcoming boxing matches. Those were fights worth reading about.

By the time I started first grade, in an area locally

known as "the meadows," I was already in the middle of an identity crisis. I kept a few close friends, and as much fun as they were, I had an unshakable feeling that I couldn't define. The only thing I knew was that I felt alone and somehow separated. There was a lingering phantom stirring in my subconscious, which I eventually discovered was called anxiety. That feeling caused me to view my teachers and classmates as potential threats, so I retreated inward where I could observe from a safe distance. I began to analyze everything I was seeing and hearing, pulling it apart into smaller digestible portions and then storing it in a mental file that I could access whenever I needed to understand what the world was doing to me.

Growing up in a predominately Irish/Italian neighborhood, most of us were sent to catholic school by default. Those who weren't ended up in Philadelphia's public schools, which were mostly substandard and carried the unfair stigma of being a hotbed for kids who would grow into irresponsible adults. Catholic school teachers tried to reinforce their superiority through discipline and a strict expectation that all students would follow rules. It was a way of controlling by fear, and it worked. We wore drab uniforms that stripped us of all individuality, and we were told to walk in straight lines. The strongest memory I have of those first years is being afraid, being nervous, having a stomach full of butterflies for no reason other than I was uncomfortable and out of place. I could never pay attention in class and I fidgeted at my desk; each day I watched the cold gray clock on the wall move in slow motion as I felt my heart rate increase to the point of cardiac arrest - at least that's what I believed.

Around this time, my mother's paranoia, which began after the abduction and murder of 6-year-old Adam Walsh in 1981, came alive because I was now close to his age. The

Walsh case had gripped the throat of every parent across the country; as a result, my mother could not fathom the idea of leaving me unattended. So, in the summer between first and second grade, I was sent to daycare at Patterson Elementary to keep me occupied and safe. I never liked the rigidness of Patterson's routine, especially the imposed nap time around midday. All of us were to lie on gym-style mats and go to sleep for what felt like six hours. Realistically, it was 30 minutes, but it was torturous. I never went to sleep. Instead, I stared at the construction paper projects lining the walls and thought about drawing, writing, and building a private little universe into which I could disappear. That sounded better to me than anything I was supposed to be learning in school.

In my mind, there was an endless parade of imagination running on all cylinders, and in the outside world, there was nothing but tasks and paperwork that would make no real difference in the grand scheme of my life. Sometimes I would raise my hand above my sleeping classmates and try to go to the bathroom just to break the monotony, but it was rarely successful. So, I listened to the clock ticking and counted to 60. *One minute.* Then, I counted to 60 again. *Two minutes.* By counting down in silence, I figured out how much time was left until we were allowed to move again - until the lights would be turned on and the afternoon came back to life.

Since my mother was working all day, Pop would pick me up from daycare. The highlight of my day at Patterson was his arrival and our James Bond-like escape. That became our thing; it was a special handshake, a secret club, and we were the only members. Although we weren't supposed to go home until late in the day, Pop would show up around noon. I vividly remember the feeling of watching the door open and knowing that it would be him on the other side. I remember his worn baseball cap, his constant, white five o'clock shadow, and the cigarette dangling from his lip as he stepped through the doorway and flashed a knowing grin, non-verbally acknowledging that we were breaking the rules.

As soon as we were out of there, he would walk me across the street to a small candy store and tell me to pick out whatever I wanted, which was usually Peanut Chews or Mary Janes, and then we were off to his house, where episodes of *The Dukes of Hazzard* filled the next few hours. Although I didn't understand the concept of the show, it represented our buddyhood and the idea that I was important because Pop made a special point of keeping me company. One day I found a *Dukes of Hazzard* t-shirt draped over the long console record player in the living room. By the time I noticed it was my size, he was already patting me on the shoulder.

"Try it on," he said. "And then let's go see what Boss Hogg is up to today."

It may have been a small gesture but rescuing me from Patterson brought light into my world when everything else felt overcast. Pop couldn't have known it at the time, but he saved me from drowning every day.

4. IMAGININGS

After living in an apartment at 65th & Greenway Avenue, where I broke my arm on the cement porch and spent a humid summer wearing a cast that would not stop itching, my mother, Rick and I moved to the corner of 71st & Dorel in 1984. We were now one block away from Pop and Gram's house, and directly across the street from St. Irenaeus Church and the massive field surrounding it.

Whenever I think about the house on Dorel, I think of the color brown. Everything in it was brown, from the carpeting to the tree-patterned wallpaper. The coffee table was cheap wood, the entertainment center was dark particleboard, and the faux leather sofa (which would eventually be torn apart and left with stuffing-filled holes) was a shade of rust. The entire structure was 936 square feet, and only about 2/3 of that was livable space. There was a large, halfway dead tree in the wraparound yard and a set of hidden steps on the side leading down to a basement entrance. To me, those were features begging to be thrust into whatever wild story I could dream up in my spare time.

Early on, I was able to sense an odd disconnect in the way our house functioned. My mother and Rick operated like independent mechanical robots, going through the motions without interacting with one another. I remember watching both of them individually and feeling confused about my role in the arrangement. There seemed to be three groups under one roof: me and my mother, me and Rick, and Rick and my mother. Each group had its own set of rules for normal behavior, or so I believed.

Rick's interaction with me was always uncomfortable, not because he did anything specific to that end (at least in the beginning), but because of my meddling inner voice that played devil's advocate in almost every situation. Since he had no children of his own, I had a hard time accepting that I was filling any void that needed to be filled, or if a void was even there. Rick never spoke about children; truthfully, I don't believe having a child mattered to him, and if it did, he was a master at covering those feelings with indifference. My mother didn't see the resistant side of Rick; I was simply an extension of her, and in her mind, Rick was just going to accept me on those grounds. But I was watching these moving parts from a different angle and I knew that Rick would have preferred that my mother had come without stipulations. I quickly became a puzzle piece with no place to fit. Yet, despite the awkwardness pervading our home, I would stay quiet and grind through the next 12 or 13 years until the law allowed me to break the door down and fade into the world on my own. That was my plan at the time, and it made sense. Until then, I just needed to stay busy so I wouldn't focus on how different I felt from everyone else.

Every night when I was supposed to go to sleep, I became jittery and on edge. My bed was positioned against the rear wall, and behind it was a window that looked out across the church field. I made a habit of sitting on my knees and resting my arms on top of the headboard as I stared into the dark expanse, waiting for anything out of the ordinary to grab my attention. Maybe I would spot a wandering 18th-century specter with a tricorn hat floating over his old farm, or perhaps the materialization of a towering castle that once occupied the land. All of these were possibilities in my mind, and I could spend hours there, with my eyes glazed over, conjuring ghosts in the moonlight.

However, there was one hallucination that always eclipsed the others. In the distance beyond the field, there was a bridge with tall suspension cables and flickering colors. When I focused hard enough, the bridge became a large cruise ship. I could visualize the passengers and other rich details, from the mandatory life rings to the evening gowns worn by the wives and girlfriends who drank champagne and giggled while their men discussed business ventures. I could hear the glasses clanging together as people toasted each other; I could smell the cigar smoke wafting toward the stars. I wanted nothing more but to escape and join the festivities. Somewhere in the back of my mind, I felt I belonged there — with the people on the ship, alive and wondrous — as a beacon on the ethereal river. I wanted to be part of them; I wanted to leave the mundane world behind and run for my life, across the field, and through the houses until I found myself at the watery threshold. From there I would grab a raft and float toward the rope ladder. It was all so simple, and yet, I was only a child. So, the partygoers would eventually drift into the night, their laughter fading to whispers, while I sank back into my pillow, heavy-eyed and brokenhearted.

When the excitement of my nocturnal phantasmagoria

ended, there was nothing for me to do but lie on my bed and stare at the ceiling, looking for constellations in the shadows. When I slept, I had odd dreams most nights.

In one dream, I had gotten out of bed to use the bathroom, but had trouble walking as soon as my feet touched the floor. Somehow, I was able to reach across the room and flick the light switch, and when I did, I saw that my carpet was covered in roaches. I felt repulsed by the sight of them and stomped repeatedly to scare them away, which worked well enough for me to reach the hallway. Once there, the sensation of metal in my throat overtook me, and I had the urge to open the closet. In waking life, this closet kept spare rolls of toilet paper and towels; in my dream, it had a splintered door and a loose knob as though it was from an abandoned house. I stared down at the knob, knowing that something was pushing me to open it, like a subconscious whispering that was neither threatening nor comforting. When I relented, a blinding light filled the hallway for more than a minute; after it subsided, I saw the face of God looking back at me, suspended in air and partially transparent. I reached my hand out but woke up calmly before I could make contact.

In another dream, I found myself walking alone in a vast French cemetery. Rows of tombstones stretched far back to the horizon and I struggled to make sense of the layout before finding a caretaker tending to the grounds. I asked him where I could find Napoleon's final resting place. The strange fact, however, was that I consciously knew Napoleon was buried indoors at *Les Invalides* in Paris, not in a common outdoor graveyard. Still, I waited for the caretaker to answer. "I can walk you over to his plot," he told me. We set off across the large field until he stopped near a small, ordinary white military stone. "Here he is. Right here." I fixated on the embossed letters rising from the surface of the marble, which spelled out Napoleon's full name in Italian. *Napoleone di Buonaparte.* As I studied the writing, I could see that the caretaker was still standing next to me and I became uncomfortable. When I turned to leave, he muttered: "Do you want to see something interesting?" Before I could answer, he knelt in front of the grave and opened a small compartment that was built-in to the stone, but invisible to the naked eye. Suddenly, a rolled piece of old paper fell from inside the opening; when the caretaker unraveled it, it bore my name.

Since that night, I have had a recurring cemetery dream at least once every few months. The cemetery appears to have differences from dream to dream, but it's the same cemetery. I know it is. There is always a famous person buried there, and sometimes there are multiple. There are sections that feel miles away from each other: a dilapidated square with old stones and overgrown brush, a tall white tower with several floors and reflective walls inside, decorative plots with many colors. I am almost always alone in those dreams, wandering, lost, searching. Even when there's daylight, it is menacing and dark.

The most prevalent and unsettling cemetery dream occurred one evening after my mother and Rick had been in a vicious argument that made me feel nervous. I tossed and turned for a while because my heart was racing and I couldn't stay calm long enough to fall asleep. It was in the middle of summer and I always kept my window opened slightly to find relief from the humidity, but that also meant that I could hear every car that drove past our house. It was after two o'clock in the morning when I drifted off and found myself outside of the cemetery office.

When I walked inside, there were rows of filing cabinets with burial records, and interments in the walls as though the office itself was one large mausoleum. A woman stood behind the front desk, talking so rapidly on the phone that I couldn't hear anything more than a loud buzzing sound. I tried hard to get her attention but she kept waving her hands like I was interrupting. When I started to speak, she covered the phone and responded before I could say anything.

"No, you can't go see those, they're off-limits," she said.

I had no idea what she meant until I looked behind her and noticed another room with a rope barricading the doorway. Beyond the rope were marble statues of Jesus Christ and different Catholic saints, which I somehow interpreted to mean that they were buried there. Beside each statue was an empty chair.

Since I had been forbidden to see the room in more detail, I wandered away from the front desk and into another room with other wall interments, which displayed the names of infamous and mythical beings. There was one intimidating marker that startled me; it read "Your Devil" and then beneath "Presumably Lucifer" with a death date and location in medieval Russia. Across the surface of the marker was the holographic image of Satan.

I walked back to the front desk; the woman, who was still on the phone, said: "Go on, I know you want to see that room, just go!" Though I thought she was referring to the room behind her with the marble statues, she was pointing to a different room on her left. It was arranged like a mid-century living room with angular furniture and a starburst clock on the wall. The sofa and chairs had deceased people sitting on them, strategically posed to look like they were alive with opaque bed sheets covering them. I quickly walked away and past the woman once more, who handed me her business card. I could see her name clearly but forgot it the moment I woke up. When I opened my eyes, I saw that it was the middle of the night. I remember feeling dread, that something was standing in the corner, quietly staring at me. To avoid looking at the corners of the room, I focused on my closet door and the chipped paint that was barely visible from the outside lights. I didn't stop watching until dawn.

Every morning, often tired from my restless nights, I would ready myself for the day without much enthusiasm. School began to feel like a punishment for being too young and having no control over my schedule. The relentlessness of Catholicism, at least in an elementary school setting, was like slow, deliberate suffocation. We were not *taught*; we were *told*. As long as we prayed to this saint or that saint, everything would be fine; as long as we confessed our sins (to other flawed human beings) we would be forgiven. Every teacher was a nun or a priest with almost no worldly knowledge aside from the experience of living in their respective convents or rectories, which were always isolated from the rest of society. They could no more prepare us for the real world than a monk could run an organized crime ring.

Once I was dressed, Rick would finish his morning routine, which consisted of packing the same lunch every single day: a tuna fish sandwich, cherry pie, and chocolate milk. Then, he would grab his umbrella and walk me across the street so I could wait for the school bus in the church parking lot. When the bus arrived and we piled on, I always sat alone, usually about midway between the center and the back. I never sat near the front because there was too much exposure, and I didn't want to sit in the back because that was too obvious and strange. I thought splitting the difference would have no definable motive, but would still afford me the result I truly wanted: total anonymity. There was so much noise in my head that adding any amount of mindless small talk would push me into overload. Plus, my classmates were shouting about Voltron, Cabbage Patch Kids, and Transformers, and I didn't care. None of it appealed to me, and that added to my solitariness because I tried to understand not only why I was uninterested, but how everyone else could easily slide into this affable mold when I could barely make eye contact.

Every two weeks, we were marched into the school library where we were told to pick a book. The teachers didn't seem to care about which books we read, as long as we were kept busy. After all, the Bible was our foundation and idleness could lead us to sin. It was better in the eyes of our clergy to fall into the animated landscape of Dr. Seuss or follow Encyclopedia Brown as he invariably solved some ridiculous mystery. My introversion wouldn't allow me to congregate with everyone else as they wrangled for control of the most popular titles. Instead, I drifted close to the bookcases on the opposite side of the room where nobody dared browse and most often chose something from the history section. While my schoolmates were clustered in packs and turning their pages much too loudly for any respectable librarian to excuse, I stayed to myself and read about John F. Kennedy and PT-109. I found solace in the history books because these stories were set in stone and unchangeable. While the unpredictability of the present and the future made me uncomfortable, here, in these books, were events in a state of permanence that I could examine without anticipatory danger. These books offered me a sense of comfort, stability, and a method of escape from the chaos around me.

Those stories of bygone people and events filled my thoughts each day as I sat in my hard, wooden desk and tried to look like I was paying attention. No matter how much I struggled to control my focus, I could not force myself to listen in class. As a result, I rarely tested well and my grades were borderline average. On occasion, I got stickers and praise on subjects that came easy to me, like English and Spelling, and that was enough to create the illusion that I was making an effort. But I knew I would rather daydream than memorize the correct way to solve a long division problem. I was not trying to deliberately buck the system; I was trying to survive the afternoon.

When the weather got colder, Rick stopped walking me to the churchyard to meet the bus, and I was fine with that. Pop would pick me up in his Skylark with a hot, covered plate of breakfast waiting on the bench seat. Gram began cooking for me every morning; most times it was scrambled eggs and toast, or chipped beef and gravy. She would put it on a plate and snap a plastic lid over it to lock in the heat, then send it out into the frigid morning with Pop to help me start my day. Sitting in that car with the radio permanently fixed on news that I was too young to care about, eating as the warm air rushed through the vents in the dashboard, gave me something to anticipate instead of panicking about Trapper Keepers and piles of loose-leaf.

Once the first few years of elementary school passed, I began staying at Pop and Gram's house after school. I was too young to warrant a key to my house, and both my mother and Rick worked until after 5 p.m. Pop took me along for the ride whenever he ran errands, including several trips to Sweeney's Fish Market on Woodland Avenue, which had no relevance to my family but felt like it did. Pop always bought smelts there. It was the only thing I ever remember him buying. When we got home, he would unwrap them and start cooking while I sat at the kitchen table, listening to his random facts like which flowers were the first to grow in springtime. *Forsythia*. That was the one he always focused on, "...because the bees love them, and bees are important." Gram saved old coffee grinds so Pop could spread them around the base of his plants as fertilizer. I didn't fully comprehend what he was telling me, but the beautiful tomatoes and watermelon he grew each summer lent enough credibility for me to pay attention.

Pop could talk for hours about nature. He loved animals, both domestic pets and the wildlife on National Geographic, which he never missed whenever he remembered to watch it. I inherited his love for all living things and routinely looked for injured birds and squirrels outside. I never knew what I would do with them once I found them, but the idea of leaving them defenseless was something that bothered me deeply. On occasion, I would find a bird that had fallen from its nest and would try to make it comfortable, usually hiding it away behind the rickety wooden doors on the alcove beneath our back porch until I could alert someone. Most of them pushed their way out because I had probably exaggerated their injuries in my zeal for doing the right thing. But one time, there was a baby finch with a broken wing that I was able to pass off to a rehabilitation center. Months later I discovered that it healed and had learned to fly.

In 1987, my mother took me to New Jersey to see my father. I had no memory of him up to that point. We met at a shopping mall in Deptford, somewhere public and in plain view, presumably as a hindrance to whatever sudden behavioral change he might have. When we pulled into the parking lot and walked inside, I was introduced to him like a neighbor I was meeting for the first time. *This is your father.* He tried to make small talk but was visibly nervous.

I was as foreign to him as he was to me, and he knew that everything he said was being monitored as though he was talking on a prison telephone.

His deep voice was frightening. He was friendly and spoke like an interested and attentive parent, but the only thing I heard in my mind was a looping dialogue of how terrible he was. I had been programmed to distrust him. When he asked me questions, I replied in one or two words. The three of us walked through the mall exchanging hollow statements until we found a music store and ducked inside, hoping there would be enough diversion to get us through the awkwardness of it all.

"Get anything you want," my father told me.

Awkward or not, there was always something exciting about a new acquisition. I studied the rows of cassette tapes for an eternity before pulling out an Iron Maiden album. I had never heard Iron Maiden but I loved the artwork on the cover. It was colorful and horrifying. I was immediately drawn to it. My father caught up to me and saw what I was holding.

"You want *that?*"

I nodded.

He nodded back.

As soon as he pulled out money to pay at the register, I saw a display of California Raisin tapes on the counter that had been arranged to promote their latest kitschy release to every kid in America.

The California Raisins Sing the Hit Songs

Four animated raisins in bow ties and wing-tipped shoes against a blue curtain, crooning hits from the 60s and 70s. The Iron Maiden tape quickly lost its appeal. Before I could say anything, the clerk was already putting the Raisin album in a bag. She handed it to me and I left the store with a smile on my face, thinking of the cassette player sitting in our basement and eagerly waiting for the chance to jam the tape inside.

That's the last thing I remember about seeing my father that day.

Years later I found out that his second wife, Bernice, forbade him to visit me because she knew that my mother would also be there. Bernice was convinced that the emotion of seeing me would elicit some old feelings in favor of family reconciliation and he would leave her. It was an irrational concern, but to avoid listening to her complaints, my father only made plans to see me when he and Bernice were fighting, because in those moments he no longer cared about throwing gasoline on her burning anger. Such was his passive-aggressive method of revenge.

I would only see him twice more.

5. ROOM FULL OF MIRRORS

Those who were around and old enough to remember the Kennedy assassination can likely tell you where they were and what they were wearing when they heard the news. In 2001, when the World Trade Center fell in the most brazen attack on the United States since Pearl Harbor, I was standing in the lobby of my workplace, staring at the television as the visibly shaken anchor tried to make sense of the updates streaming into her earpiece.

None of this sounds particularly impressive, but it appears to illustrate a universal truth about memory and its relationship to places in time. In fact, psychologists have hypothesized that we store memories according to *where* they happened, and that the details of our surroundings become more pertinent if something significant occurred there. For instance, I could walk into a room and notice the arrangement of the furniture, the photos on the wall, and the texture of the carpet; but, without any added stimuli, it becomes a memory in the abstract and will eventually dim until I can no longer recall it. Conversely, if

I had walked into that same room and taken notice of the surroundings before hearing an explosion across the street, the specifics would be further ingrained because of their relationship to a more distinctive event. This phenomenon even has a name: Episodic Memory Formation.

There was an aura in Pop and Gram's house that I've never been able to put into words. Every attempt I've made has fallen short in some way, and maybe it's because, as a reality, it could only have existed when it did. When I remember it now, I see it through a blurred lens with muffled sounds, like a memory that's strong enough to still be present, but distant enough to be stolen by the passing years. But some of my recollections are so vivid that I can feel their house rebuilding itself around me.

At Christmas, it was a reflection of habit and thriftiness; decorations long past their prime were pushed into every crevice, and the revolving color wheel originally used to bounce light off the aluminum tree they had decades before, still turned despite a missing panel and no real practicality. There was always a plastic Santa taped to the inside of the front door and bright garland snaking through every opening, intertwined with multi-colored bulbs that danced around the room to create a holiday discotheque. It looked like Christmas had exploded and I loved it because there was something protective about that environment. Somehow the covered walls and the smell of their coffee, mixed with the sound of Gram's daytime soap operas in one room and Pop's old sitcoms in the other, provided a feeling of warmth. Maybe those things represented normalcy to me.

In the summer, their house was completely different. The screen door was all that separated us from the outside world and the sound of gas lawnmowers roared all day long. Almost every window was open because of the humidity. Gram would make her famous gallon of iced tea from the powdered mix they kept in the cabinet; and somehow, it complimented the supply of geometrically-shaped Little Debbie cakes that were always on hand.

Pop and Gram had a gray radio/cassette player on their kitchen counter. Most times it was permanently tuned to a Country station because it reminded them of their livelier days with friends. But every so often, Pop would sit in his dining room chair and twist the dial through many rounds of static and intermittent broadcasts until something caught his ear. One of my strongest episodic memories is Pop fiddling with the radio and then placing it on the kitchen table once he settled on a particular song. It was a warm Saturday morning in June and Gram was still in her nightgown. Pop scooted his chair back and walked over to Gram, putting one hand around her waist and taking her hand in his other. They danced in a circle as Gram hummed along to the melody coming from the radio. The music was romantic and haunting (years later I identified it as *Sleepwalk* by Santo and Johnny); I sat on the floor with my legs crossed watching them move like teenagers. "We used to do this every weekend," Pop said to me. "In those days everybody went out dancin'," Gram added in her thick city accent. I just smiled.

On days when there was no school, I planted myself on their couch by 8 a.m. and watched reruns of *The Little Rascals*. I became so engrossed in black and white television shows (which not only brought history to life but also felt mysterious through the poor reception of rabbit ears) that I wanted to quit school and exist solely in another era. My room was a kaleidoscope of strange interests, which included scattered drawings of historical figures on used envelopes, and copies of The Declaration of Independence and The Constitution printed on sheets purposely made to look like they had survived a flood. I had books stacked in piles according to category and VHS tapes that I cataloged by taping numbers to the spine and then listing those numbers in a homemade booklet with their corresponding titles.

The underlying fact was that I could not tame my anxiety at home any more than I could ignore it at school. I kept myself busy with solitary organizational tasks that allowed me to tune out my surroundings so I could continue my internal monologue. Rick spent every day consumed with his own tasks and my mother focused on working toward her goal of complete financial independence. Since I had developed a habit of never speaking up, my personal conflicts were known only to me and I started to believe that nobody would understand them anyway. I learned to avoid bothersome situations by mastering diversion. Rather than try to explain my discomfort in the hopes of overcoming it, I would define the result I wanted in my mind (like staying home from school) and reverse engineer the process of getting there with the least amount of resistance from anyone else who needed to be involved. I mapped out different scenarios and then calculated the likely response to each one. If I encountered a "brick wall" (a term I adopted to describe being asked a follow-up question I couldn't answer), I would scrap the plan and go back to the beginning. As I recall this now, it just sounds like elaborate lying; at the time, it was a method of self-preservation.

I remember one occasion where I failed a test miserably. I never tested well because I couldn't retain information that I considered uninteresting. No matter how many times I studied facts and statements, I could not keep them in my brain. I could have rattled off the Gettysburg Address more easily than passing a five-question science quiz. The problem was that all tests, good or bad, had to be signed by a parent. When I received my failed test with the added insult of the teacher's crudely-drawn unhappy face in the top right corner, I began devising ways to have it signed by my mother without her seeing it. I immediately thought of the canceled checks she kept in the drawer of her bedroom computer desk. There were probably hundreds of them, all bearing her meticulous signature with almost no variation in pressure or letter formation. Every time she signed her name, it looked like a stamp. It still does.

When there was no risk of being seen, I took one of the checks into my room. Then, I placed my test beneath it to trace over her signature with enough force to leave an indentation, which I could go back and fill in with a pen. But tracing the letters with a pencil would leave remnants of graphite on the check's surface, and I was too nervous that my mother would notice it someday and demand an explanation - most likely from me. Instead, I found a clickable pen and made sure that the point was not out; then, I angled it so that only the edge of the pen's rim touched the check. That allowed me to achieve the same effect without any residual evidence. Once I had a debossed version of the signature, I completed my fraudulent masterpiece. The downside was that Rick noticed my actions through the doorway and stuck around long enough for me to finish. He said nothing, but walked away with a knowing grin that told me he would use that act of defiance to his advantage in the near future.

When I was about nine years old, I became the target of a bully. Another student in my class with a penchant for breaking the rules and irking the nuns was told that I insulted his mother. Of course, I hadn't, but the rumor was enough to set him off and he tormented me for months.

At first, I was too meek to retaliate so I looked for ways to get out of school. I decided to capitalize on my mother's paranoia that something would happen to me by faking a severe illness. For a few nights straight, I complained of stomach pains. Then one morning while she was getting ready for work in the bathroom, I slipped down to the kitchen and filled my mouth with ketchup and water - just enough to thin the consistency. After swishing it around, I ran back upstairs and made sure to "vomit blood" in front of her. As I predicted, she panicked and rushed me to the doctor, where I did a barium swallow so they could examine my upper gastrointestinal tract. The results came back normal (as I knew they would), but my mother allowed me to stay home a few days for observation. That meant breakfast, blankets, and classic television at Pop and Gram's house. On days when I was unable to convince my mother that I was sick, facing the endless bullying actually *made* me sick. The moment I walked into the hallway and started passing the wooden classroom doors and cotton ball and crayon art projects, my stomach began to turn like a rusted, archaic machine. Every minute felt like an eternity, every hour a deeper plunge into the complex hatred I had for my own diffidence.

Finally, I realized that I had taken enough abuse.

My bully, who inconveniently sat directly behind me, decided that he would start picking on me every time the teacher turned her back. He poked me in the neck with pencils, hit me in the spine with his knuckle, and pulled hairs on my head until he did it one time too many. Every feeling of retaliation I had withheld came to the surface as I turned around, grabbed him by the shirt and threw him into the next row of desks with all of my strength. The teacher ran up the aisle towards us, but before she could intervene, I was already standing over top of him with a balled fist and a rage that had boiled over into action. He was visibly terrified; the other students, who had known me as reserved and passive, were struggling to comprehend what they had seen. I had acted so hastily that I failed to consider any of the consequences, and before I knew it, both of us were sitting in front of the principal. Luckily for me, my pristine disciplinary record against his pattern of detentions was enough to work in my favor. I was sent back to class and his parents were called. The following day he wouldn't even look in my direction, and he never bothered me again.

That weekend I sat on the floor against my bed and thought about the change in my behavior, wondering if it was permanent or a momentary lapse of reason. It wasn't enough that it felt good to turn the tables; I had to know why. My switch from a reticent shadow to someone who fought back was too abrupt to be random. Maybe I wasn't the person I thought I was; maybe there was someone else buried under my fragile self-confidence. In one moment, the frustration I had suppressed for so long overpowered my intellect and I acted solely on emotion. Could I go to school without discomfort from that point forward? I didn't know. I felt the same, and yet, there was some part of me that had just broken down a wall.

A few months prior I had started reading a book on Rene Descartes. I got about halfway through and abandoned it because it dealt heavily with math, the subject I hated most. But the book also told of his struggle with perception and the trustworthiness of his own senses, based on how vividly he dreamed. It described a dream he had in which he was sleeping by a roaring fire and could feel the physical heat against his skin from the flames. He subsequently questioned how he could believe what was real if he could experience the same feelings in a dream that he could while awake.

That level of analysis appealed to me and I started using my imagination to comb through my own mysteries. Maybe everything that made me anxious, all of those dangerous specters weighing me down, maybe, maybe those things didn't really exist. If they were fictitious, there was a chance I could kill them for good. I would close my eyes and picture the inside of my mind as a large white room. Then, I would place my issue on a chair in the center of that room. Around the perimeter, one by one, I watched as different people I admired faded into view. They were people from history, most from hundreds of years ago. I would listen as they offered their opinions (or what I assumed their opinions would be) on the issue. In some odd way, it often led me to an answer, and if it didn't, it made the subject too tiring to think about anymore.

But the major fears that plagued me were too strong to banish with a simple flick of reverse psychology. I felt extremely isolated from other people. When I received birthday gifts or compliments, I didn't feel like I deserved them. Moreover, I never consciously believed any compliment I was paid, even if I knew it to be true subconsciously.

Much of my time, when I wasn't putting my possessions in alphabetical order, was spent consumed by art. I began drawing day and night - faces, expressions, and complex shapes with shading for added depth. I admired M.C. Escher, particularly his 1953 sketch *Relativity*, and I tried endlessly to replicate his style. I tore through photo books of Salvador Dali's work and became obsessed with examining his painting, *The Persistence of Memory*. I wanted to figure that painting out, but I knew there was no true explanation; ironically, it was the thing I loved most. It meant whatever anyone wanted it to mean, and it had no meaning at all. Both were correct. It didn't have to fit in a box. Surrealism taught me that it was okay to view the world differently.

Pop lauded my artwork. Anytime I completed a new drawing, I would show it to him and he would always reply the same way. "You're really talented, you can really draw!" For emphasis, he would lean over into Gram's ear and ask, "Did you see his drawing, Em?" She would nod yes and smile. And I believed them; I believed that they were actually proud of something I had accomplished. But they were the only people I trusted to be honest. If anyone else made the same comment, I pushed it out of my mind. *They're just saying that.*

Gram took more photographs than anyone I have ever known. She was great about labeling each of her photos with the subject and date. As I sat in their living room one afternoon scanning through photos to draw, I came across one of a man I had never seen before. He was shabbily dressed with a blank look on his face. There was no writing on the back of the photo.

"Who's this?" I asked.

"That's Billy, my brother Billy," Pop replied.

I was caught off guard. Pop had a brother. I couldn't understand why he had never been mentioned. Pop didn't keep secrets from me. The whole situation was confusing. Before I could ask anything else, he said: "He's afflicted."

"What do you mean?"

Gram took over.

"Billy was dropped as a baby, down a flight of steps. It was an accident, but it hurt him and he can't take care of himself. He's in a home with other people who need the same kind of help."

Eventually, I learned that Billy had never been dropped, but was simply born with a mental disability. Pop's parents, presumably to hide some level of shame over their disadvantaged child, devised a cover story that nobody bothered to question, including Pop and Gram.

I also learned that, prior to 1972, public schools were allowed to deny enrollment to children deemed "uneducable" (largely those with intellectual disabilities), despite a state law that required all children to attend school. As an alternative, parents with disabled children were urged to send them to institutions that were better equipped to handle their needs. Many of those institutions purposely rebranded themselves as a "school" to reassure the public that they were acting in the children's best interest.

This explained why, by the age of 17, Billy was sent to Pennhurst State School and Hospital (originally the Eastern Pennsylvania Institution for the Feeble-Minded and Epileptic) in Spring City, Pennsylvania, where he was labeled an "inmate". Pennhurst was once considered a model of professionalism but was already grossly overcrowded years before Billy's arrival due to the admittance of adult immigrants, orphans, criminals, and anyone else deemed abnormal by societal standards. He spent years wasting away in Pennhurst, unable to communicate clearly enough with his parents to explain the horrible ways he was being treated. Pennhurst's staff, meanwhile, presented themselves as caring and thoughtful. It wasn't until Pop visited Billy one day that the truth emerged. Billy had been beaten so severely by his caretakers that he nearly lost an eye. Pop immediately took him out of Pennhurst and placed him in a more private setting.

Years later, in 1971, the Pennsylvania Association for Retarded Citizens (now the Arc of PA) sued the Commonwealth of Pennsylvania over the law that gave public schools the authority to deny a free education to children who had reached the age of 8, yet had not reached the mental age of 5. The case, which lasted a year, was the first major legal case to provide equality to students with disabilities and was finally settled early in 1972 when "a consent decree was given by the U.S. District Court Judge Masterson who ruled the existing law restricting kids ages six to twenty-one years of age was unconstitutional. It was also stated that Pennsylvania was responsible for providing free public education to all children; that meant that no child, regardless of their disability, could be turned down by the Commonwealth to the access of free public trainings and educational programs. The quality of the education and training given to the children with disabilities had to match that of the education and training given to general students."

The decision to sue over the right to education was motivated in part by concerns about conditions at Pennhurst and the fear that children who were barred from attending school were more likely to end up in an institution.

On a federal level, the Rehabilitation Act of 1973, enacted a year after the Pennsylvania case, prohibited discrimination on the basis of disability in programs conducted by federal agencies, in programs receiving federal financial assistance, in federal employment and in the employment practices of federal contractors. Specifically, Section 504 stated:

No otherwise qualified individual with a disability in the United States, as defined in section 705 (20) of this title, shall, solely by reason of his or her disability, be excluded from the participation in, be denied the benefits of, or be subjected to discrimination under any program or activity receiving Federal financial assistance or under any program or activity conducted by any Executive agency or by the United States Postal Service.

Sadly, the progress came too late for Billy, who had already suffered years of abuse in several institutions and never received an education.

Pop and Billy had one other sibling, a sister named Helen, who had moved to Florida years earlier and rarely had any contact with her side of the family. Helen was also a bit more well off than Pop but never offered to help with the financial strain of Billy's care. As a result, Billy was moved from one facility to another, either because his caretakers could no longer deal with him or because his care had become too expensive. Every so often, Pop and Gram would fill a box with candy, trinkets, and activities and take them to Billy. On one occasion, they brought him a simple, inexpensive wristwatch, which could've been a Rolex by how proudly he showcased it to his fellow patients. In a building full of childlike adults, Billy now owned something that excited him. Later, it was discovered that other people in the facility would beat and punch Billy before stealing the items he was given. His candy was stolen and the watch was never seen again.

Though I had not met Billy at that point, something about the cruelty he suffered hurt me on two different levels. I felt a sensation in my body that was not physical, but full of pain. And for some reason, my brain would search its archives for sad music I had heard and begin looping it as a backdrop to the troubling thoughts I was having. In effect, I was creating a soundtrack to other people's misery and torturing myself involuntarily. Then, I felt even more sorry for Pop, who had done his best for an ailing brother, only to see those efforts crushed by the rottenness of humanity.

6. AND MILES TO GO

I became too old for Patterson's daycare services after a while, so Pop and I spent a lot of time fishing in the summer. The first thing we did each year was walk to Taylor's Bait and Tackle so Pop could renew his fishing license. I remember his old, raggedy tackle box; it looked like he had been using it since the 1960s and had never bothered to untangle the fishing line from the several red and white bobbers thrown in haphazardly.

There was a hidden pond not too far away, steeped in just enough shade to ward off the heat. But because we lived in the city and Pop hadn't driven long distances in some time, the pond was still spitting distance from the road and the occasional sound of traffic noise. It was the only detraction from an otherwise perfect setting. The trees lining the edge of the water guaranteed I would find a V-shaped branch that I could burrow into the mud to use as a pole stand.

As soon as we arrived, Pop would leave both of his car

doors open and start unloading our supplies, which included the requisite equipment, a couple of sandwiches from Gram, an old Coleman cooler full of ice water, and sliced up pieces of a hot dog. Pop always used hot dogs or pieces of chicken on his hooks; he was convinced it was vastly superior to live bait, a theory fine by me since it meant not having to kill worms.

He always brought a fedora-shaped straw hat with a built-in sun visor and gave me one of his baseball caps to wear, which was predictably too large and slid down over my eyes. But Pop also knew that I was sensitive to brightness and that direct sunlight made my eyes water uncontrollably, so he made sure that we never went on an outing without something to keep me protected.

We rarely caught anything, but I realize now that it wasn't ever about fishing. Pop used that time to reminisce about his childhood in Ambler, Pennsylvania (roughly 30 miles northeast of Southwest), and how the open fields would ripple far into the distance. He took notice of small nuances around him like the smell of certain plants and flowers, and he would do his best to describe them to me so I would be able to detect them on my own. I heard about his mandolin picking as a young man (a skill clearly inherited from his father) and how much he wished he had still had one to play. I made a promise to myself that I would find a way to give him one someday.

The thing he missed the most, evident from the sheer amount of times he brought it up, was the Perkiomen Creek in Montgomery County. There was something about its tranquility that called him; as a boy, he would fish or just relax on the rocks and watch the surface of the water flow past him.

Every so often he would bring up Midvale. "I made the guns for World War II," he would say. He was still proud of his machinery skills and the decades he spent making sure everything he touched was a testament to his perfectionism. And even though there was no denying the satisfaction he took in recalling those years, there was also no mistaking the underlying hint of disappointment in his voice. Despite the loss against Midvale around the time of my mother's elopement (and the fact that Pop had given up hope for compensation), it was still a lingering blow that haunted him as an unfinished chapter in his life. He had been pushed into retirement before he was ready, and had nothing to show for his work aside from the dark blue t-shirts he still occasionally wore with oil spots that were too embedded to be washed out.

Unfortunately, the Pension Benefit Guaranty Corporation settled a landmark case later, in April 1987, that would have restored 65% of Pop's full pension with interest, since he had been one of the thousands of workers whose plans were terminated between 1976 and 1981. However, he was still ineligible for not having reached the age of 62.

When Pop and I weren't fishing, we drove around to different stores to kill time. Everyone at the local grocery store knew him on a first-name basis because he struck up conversations with unsuspecting people. On one such afternoon, we walked into Shop N Bag and he immediately headed toward the fruit and vegetable section. I followed closely behind as he maneuvered through carts to reach a display of honeydew melons, which he thought were God's gift to nutrition. And while I'm sure he was interested in buying a few, it became clear that he was also interested in trying to impress the blonde woman standing there with a basket slung over her arm.

"These are great!" he said, pointing to the display. "Do you know how many vitamins are in honeydew?"

The woman smiled politely and tried to answer, but Pop had more to say.

"Vitamin C...great for the skin. Also has a lot of fiber."

I looked around, unsure of what to do while he was attempting to school her on healthy eating habits. I knew that there was nothing inappropriate about the situation; Pop craved interaction because he and Gram had been together so long that there was little to talk about anymore, and Gram was usually engrossed in *Days of Our Lives* anyway. They traded harmless jabs every so often; she would shout "Oh for God's sake, Bruce!" whenever he did something that she considered moronic, and he wouldn't hesitate to call her an ass if he thought she was behaving like one. They had essentially become the R-rated Fred and Ethel Mertz. Whenever they hit a stalemate in the argument, Gram would either shut down and go back to her television show, or Pop would say "Oh go shit in your hat!" In either case, they would act as nothing had happened five minutes later.

Pop's voice and the blonde woman faded back to the forefront of my mind.

"Well, how much do you weigh?" Pop asked her.

I hadn't heard the build-up to that question, but I could see that the woman was mortified as Pop stood there smiling, actually waiting for her to answer. It was yet another faux pas that he hadn't bothered to consider beforehand.

Around this time, I began having what I can only describe as hyper-sensory experiences. They were momentary, but some lasted for 30-60 seconds. Nothing provoked them; they would happen in an instant, and the most pervasive effect was disbelief that I was really there. While staring at something random, everything would blur in my peripheral vision as I became more focused on the object. From there, all sounds disappeared and I would feel a rush of adrenaline surging through my body while some mechanism in my brain continually attempted to prove that I existed. I did not feel like I was present; I felt detached from my body as though I was standing behind myself, speaking aggressively in my own ear.

I can't believe I'm here. I'm not here, am I? I am here. Why does it feel like I'm not here?

When the sensation ended, I would feel tired and relieved, but anxious. I also found myself bothered by certain imagery like a swarm of ants or clusters of holes, and noises like people coughing, sniffing, chewing, or biting into loud foods. I hated the feeling of tags inside my shirt, the textures of certain things I ate, and specific patterns of lighting. Repetitive sounds (especially those I couldn't stop), such as a dripping faucet or someone tapping their foot, would fill me with such unease that I would cover my ears and rock back and forth.

Though not officially diagnosed (and I'm not self-diagnosing), my symptoms fit nearly all the criteria for Sensory Modulation Disorder, one of the three subtypes of Sensory Processing Disorder that deals with over-responsiveness to certain visual, auditory, and tactile stimuli. It is considered by some to be part of the Autism spectrum. The STAR Institute for Sensory Processing Disorder defines this pattern in the following way:

> *Individuals with sensory over-responsivity are more sensitive to sensory stimulation than most people. Their bodies feel sensation too easily or too intensely. They might feel as if they are being constantly bombarded with information. Consequently, these people often have a "fight or flight" response to sensation, e.g. being touched unexpectedly or loud*

noise, a condition sometimes called "sensory defensiveness." They may try to avoid or minimize sensations, e.g. withdraw from being touched or cover their ears to avoid loud sounds.

These issues made home life a bit more unbearable, especially because Rick had a habit of clicking his teeth together while he talked. He did it purposely at the end of sentences as if he was accenting a point or sending Morse code out into the universe. He also kept his money in a clip and would rhythmically bang the corner of it on different surfaces for no apparent reason. Sometimes, I would mimic the sound more loudly so I could drown it out. When I had no way to escape the noise, I would close myself away in my room and wait, hours if necessary, until things were quiet again.

I distracted myself by cleaning the house, which was an admittedly strange pastime for a kid but also mindless and required nothing but tunnel vision. It was my version of wearing horse blinders. I started by dusting the coffee table and wiping off the entertainment center. Then, I worked on arranging the different piles of newspapers and magazines that nobody would throw away. Rick kept stacks of sports cards in plastic cases on the back end of the dining room table, and I tried my best to organize them without him realizing it. He also ate on paper plates most of the time and carelessly left them sitting around, which drove me crazy. I think the urge to clean was my way of finding order because I felt so out of control in every other aspect of my life. Unfortunately, anything I cleaned would be undone the following day. Rick enjoyed unorganized chaos; he maintained several "nests" around the house, all of which he would protect from being disturbed.

Things were becoming increasingly tense between my

mother and Rick. The reason she and my father did not work out was that he wanted to rule the castle and she would not be a kept woman. In her own way, my mother also needed control, which conflicted with my father's sense of order. But Rick's matter-of-factness was equally difficult since he cared about nothing, and his lack of a reaction was just as bad as an overreaction. He wasn't bothered that my mother was annoyed, and my mother didn't see the unfairness in expecting him to be someone other than who he was.

Their impasse began to draw a line through the center of the house; one half belonged to Rick for him to live as he saw fit, and the other half became my mother's laboratory, where she started crafting an 8-year long path to divorce. Meanwhile, I stayed out of the way. Because I lived with both of them, I was careful not to appear like I was taking sides.

When Rick and I were home by ourselves, he used my anxiety as a weapon to control me. He needed solitude when he did anything; something as simple as watching television required him to be alone. This prompted him to demand my absence by telling me to stay in my room. It wasn't disciplinary because I spent most of my time there anyway, but it always seemed to happen when I wanted to be downstairs. On the rare occasion I would argue with him (which wasn't an argument as much as it was me asking for a reason), he would threaten to tell my mother about the time he caught me forging her signature on my test.

No matter how many times he made that threat, it always worked. I was scared of my mother finding out about the forgery, mostly because Catholic school tuition was expensive and I felt as though I would be reprimanded for wasting money (since I knew how meticulous she had become with budgeting). It also had the secondary effect of preventing me from telling her about Rick's behavior; if she knew and confronted him about it - he would tell her about the forgery. It was a catch 22. In reality, she may not have had the response I feared, but I had already decided that the risk wasn't worth it and complied with Rick's instructions.

Aside from the hours I stirred upstairs against my will, there was one particular act of dominance that Rick carried out several times, again, when only he and I were home. It was an effective trigger for both my anxiety and my visual imagination, which, when coupled, caused me panic attacks.

I started to get used to Rick and his brand of justice. Do something he didn't like, however innocent, and get banished to another floor. It became an amusing routine after a while. Fortunately, he wasn't a physical authority; he preferred to give orders and liked the idea of someone not having the ability to refuse. But he could only force me to go upstairs so many times before the allure began to fade. I wasn't throwing myself on the floor in protest and I suppose it wasn't enough for him to be in charge; he needed to know that I was upset because that somehow made his punishment more valid.

When sending me upstairs wouldn't suffice, he would place a simulated telephone call (note: given my age, I believed it was real) to a group of hooded figures he called "The Ebonites." They were 15-20 feet tall and dressed in solid black, aside from a muted glow in their eyes. Because I was misbehaving (read: not exhibiting the level of subordination he wanted), Rick instructed them to pull me out of bed and through the window in the middle of the night, after which I would be blindfolded and taken away.

This had a two-part aftermath.

Screaming and crying uncontrollably, feeling my heart banging against the inside of my chest as I pictured these looming, monstrous beings floating past my window in the silence of night, I would beg Rick to hang up the phone. When he would see my face reddening and the tears running down my face, he would cover the receiver and ask "Okay, you gonna be good?!" When I swore and promised to do whatever I was told, Rick would act like he was thinking, and then say "It's too late, they're already on their way." I would continue to scream and plead until my throat hurt; and just when I was at the end of my voice, he would hang up.

Even then, I was convinced they were coming for me, and Rick would try to reassure me that he hadn't given them the address. I was in such a state of hysteria that I couldn't speak properly and my words would come out choppy and in-between shallow breaths. Rick found this comical. As I struggled to regain my composure, he laughed.

Still hyperventilating, I would go to bed and lie awake all night, too afraid to fall asleep. Every time I heard a noise outside, my heart jumped and my body shook. The Ebonite phone call was probably Rick's most effectual weapon. He used it no less than 10 times.

Even now it feels awkward to admit, but despite these troubling episodes, things weren't always bad at home. Rick's eccentricities could be appealing every once in a while. He would sometimes frequent an outdoor flea market roughly twenty minutes from our house that only operated in the winter. On nights when my mother was either working late or meeting with other members of the Women's International Trade Association (a group that worked to promote the professional advancement of women in international trade and business), Rick would take me along. I remember the smell of kerosene heaters and the bright raging fire that shot out of a trashcan near the first vendor. As Rick went in search of an item that would turn a profit, I always wandered around until I discovered something old that would allow my imagination to run away. Once, it was a *Photoplay* magazine from the 1940s. I stood alone, transfixed on the clothing and hairstyles of classic Hollywood stars, trying to imagine life in another time while the people around me blew warm breath into their hands and negotiated for a lower price on glassware and homemade jewelry.

Still, when we weren't digging through musty piles of randomness, there was a distance between me and Rick that would never be shortened. In the long term, his cold behavior left me with residual damage. I began to distrust people, not individually, but collectively. People, I surmised, were inherently self-serving and would stop at nothing to advance their own agendas, even if it meant hurting someone else to do it. Rick became a psychological predator once he knew I was susceptible to being terrified into submission. And if my stepfather could do that, what would stop a complete stranger from doing it?

Unfortunately, my distrust of people began to manifest as generalized cynicism. I started looking for inconsistencies in ordinary things; when I found them, they confirmed what I believed. One example was the toy commercials that were run ad nauseam during cartoons. On the surface, it seemed like there was an entire market dedicated to making children happy. But I looked beyond that and decided that the real goal of these toy companies was to make money. In effect, they didn't really care about kids, or if kids even enjoyed playing with the toys they were selling. The CEO may not have even had children. In my mind, that hidden motive echoed the lack of sincerity found in most of society. How could I ever be sure what was real and what was a lie?

I understood the philosophy of Rene Descartes even more; he believed that human intellect was reliable since it was created by God, and that God assigned the mind-body relationship to be conducive to our physical well-being. But the one problem I found was that people made *intellectual* choices and *moral* choices, and the morality aspect is where human beings failed each other. All of my cynical thoughts were based on the amorality of others, and because I was using my intellect to detect that amorality, it stood to reason that I was right and they were wrong. Plus, Catholicism taught me that humans are given free will, which meant they had the capacity to choose good or evil in their lives. But it also taught me that while humans were created in the image of God, they will always be imperfect. I couldn't reconcile all of the inconsistencies and circular logic in a way that explained it adequately, so I left it alone.

In my mind, Pop and Gram were always separate from the rest of society. Whatever ills existed in the world and could be perpetrated by the human race were *outside* of them. But with everyone else, my first response to anything I was told became doubt. It was better to doubt and be pleasantly surprised if I was wrong than to assume the best and be disappointed. This meant that I was always on red alert, waiting for the other shoe to drop. All good fortune was a mirage and would eventually vanish when I got close enough to touch it.

Somehow, despite not really knowing him, I had become my father.

7. RADIO SILENCE

I was 11 years old when Pop was in a minor car accident. In the process of looking over the damage, a mechanic told him that his '71 Skylark needed other work that was too expensive for someone living on Social Security. The car was towed back to the house as an interim solution until he could figure out how to scrape together extra money, all the while vowing it was only a matter of time before he would be behind the wheel again.

The larger problem was that he was in his mid-70s and starting to slow down. Even if his car had been fixed the same day, it would have only delayed the inevitable. Instead, it sat by the curb for almost a year, dripping oil and collecting stains from the birds on the overhead telephone wires.

Pop never drove again, but that didn't stop him from being mobile. Anytime they needed something from the store, he readily obliged because it was preferable to sitting around with his Captain Black cigars, reading the newspaper to the slapping sound of Gram's playing cards.

But in true fashion, a trip to the store was never just a trip to the store.

Gram played the lottery like it was a religion. She also won more than anyone I've ever known, though the winnings were always small and usually insignificant. But every so often she would take a shot at the major jackpots, and on one such occasion chose seven numbers at random for Pop to submit. He returned a half-hour later with an apple pie and cut a piece before sitting on the couch to watch *The Streets of San Francisco*.

That evening, Gram sat at the table waiting for the drawing. As the announcer started to speak, she pulled out a small piece of paper containing the numbers she had chosen earlier in the day and checked them against the ones being suctioned into the plastic tube on her TV screen. Thirty seconds later she sprang out of her chair and screamed.

She had chosen all seven numbers and won several million dollars. Pop rushed into the dining room still holding his apple pie to see what the commotion was about. When she finally regained enough composure to apprise him of their good fortune, he went blank, and Gram's smile slowly drifted downwards as her mind processed the look on his face into the only thing it could've meant.

He never played the numbers.

To remedy the situation (and perhaps to snap Gram out of her shock-induced fog), Pop went down to the basement and started working on a homemade solution. He dug through his piles of project remnants until finding a large block of wood to run across his table saw and turn into a perfect square. Once that was complete, he set the lid of a Country Crock container against the wood and traced a circle, around which he painted random numbers that he conjured out of thin air. Finally, he stuck his hand in a box of painting supplies and retrieved one of the many free stirrers he had gotten with each purchase at Barlow's Hardware Store.

Flipping the switch on a loud machine he kept bolted to his work table in the backroom, Pop fashioned one end of the paint stirrer into a point and then nailed it to the wooden block, essentially creating a rudimentary wheel of fortune that would place their next windfall in the hands of fate. When Gram saw this invention, she rolled her eyes and went back to her crossword puzzle. But Pop would not be discouraged; he swore that his stroke of genius would pay off. She would see, soon enough, he told himself.

A few months later Gram decided to play the big one again, and Pop convinced her to let him spin the wheel instead of picking numbers out of a hat. She exhaled impatiently as he plucked the sharpened paint stirrer with his middle finger and watched it land on seven different numbers, writing each down in his pocket-sized notepad. When he was done, he pushed the wooden block aside and stood up, holding the pad in the air like it contained directions to the Holy Grail. Gram paid him no mind as he walked out the door.

Hours passed and Pop was engrossed in the Daily News; Gram turned the loud dial on their little TV to the correct channel and sat in her chair, chewing nervously on a pen cap. One by one, the lottery numbers were delivered by the announcer with fervor, and after each one, Gram's eyes widened a little more. Then she sprang up again and started screaming.

Pop had done it. He and his stone-age creation had somehow chosen all seven numbers correctly and made them instant millionaires; and this time, Gram knew, it was real. Money would now be plentiful; their world was about to change. No longer would they spend their lives sitting at the dining room table, lapping away the hours with mundane activities while the excitement of a rich life passed them by. She danced around the kitchen like a schoolgirl, humming some indiscernible song from the 1930s in a fit of unbridled joy. They were wealthy beyond comprehension.

It would have been a story for the ages, had the look on Pop's face not told her, once again, that her celebration was in vain.

He hadn't played the numbers.

Although Gram was angry and frustrated, and Pop was in the proverbial dog house, I marveled at their ability to put these small wars behind them. I had seen fights between married couples that dragged on endlessly, some even becoming physical before transitioning into resentful silence and then eventually fizzling out. But Pop and Gram knew each other well enough to recognize the imperfect nature of marriage; it gave me hope, but most importantly, it assured me that they would always be together.

Because short trips to the shopping center around the corner were the extent of Pop's travels, my mother and Rick decided to make a weekly habit of taking him to see a movie every Sunday. At that point, Gram preferred to stay home and play solitaire. Whenever there was a family event, she would become the life of the party. But in everyday life, she was beginning to appreciate solitude. The closest theater was in Yeadon; it was an old 820-seat independent palace constructed in 1937 that showed second-run features for $1 per person. Just before the matinee, we would pile into Rick's car and drive 15 minutes to the edge of Delaware County.

My mother also began taking Pop to see his brother

Billy at a home-based facility in Northeast Philadelphia. It had been a few years since Pop visited and I imagine he felt guilty about leaving Billy alone with strangers, despite Billy's inability to realize that. On one of these visits, I went along. The first thing I remember is walking into a room and seeing Billy on the edge of his bed with his back turned to us. When a woman at the facility alerted him to our presence, he turned and broke into a huge smile.

"My daddy! My daddy is here! Look, my daddy!" he said.

He had mistaken Pop for their father Lawrence, who had died in 1951. Pop tried to calm Billy, but I was startled by his sudden burst of excitement because he was yelling loudly and I wasn't sure how to predict his behavior. He settled down soon after and began eating a jelly donut, half of which ended up on his shirt. I'm not sure he ever noticed me in the room.

About the time we began our Sunday trips to the movies with Pop, I was approached by one of my teachers who had taken it upon herself to recruit me for an in-class presentation. She was one of the few teachers in the school who wasn't a nun. Somehow, she took notice of my odd reading choices and decided that I would enjoy standing under the proverbial spotlight while acting out a scene from Edgar Allan Poe's *The Tell-Tale Heart*. The idea terrified me. I didn't like attention, and I hated being pushed into inescapable circumstances. When I asked why I was being singled out, she tried to reassure me that it wasn't a punishment, but a compliment, as I was the only student she thought capable of handling the text.

I still didn't understand the reason behind the performance.

Why did it have to take place at all?

After class that day, she explained that there was a

citywide prose competition for elementary school students. Each school was supposed to vet their own students and choose one to represent them. I was chosen before anyone else was considered, though up to that point, I had never touched Poe's work. I did my best to prepare for the inevitable by reading the short story multiple times; the premise concerned a narrator explaining a murder he/she had committed while also trying to convince the audience of their sanity. I walked around my bedroom miming the visual actions I believed accurately represented the words; when it came time to mimic the beating heart, I stomped my foot, knowing the effect would be greater on our wooden school floors.

The day I was scheduled to read my excerpt, I woke up in the middle of a panic attack and spent the next few hours hyperventilating. My throat felt like something was blocking it. I visualized a room of bored classmates staring at me because they either wouldn't understand my interpretation of the story or didn't care. I lent more credibility to the latter. Every other day in my scholastic career had dragged along slowly; as I anticipated, that day moved at the speed of light all the way up to the moment I was standing in front of the blackboard, glancing nervously at the directional notes I had left on the edge of the teacher's desk.

I swallowed hard and tried to remember the first line.

My assignment was not to recite the whole story, but a small portion leading to a major plot point. And still, I was struggling to begin. I had gone over these words a million times. How could they have suddenly disappeared from memory?

The only thing I could focus on was the laughter, the inevitable laughter that would follow my complete failure. I was not in a room of peers; it was a prison of embarrassment and the teacher was the warden. I couldn't just give up and run out into the halls. Everything would be waiting for me the next day, everything and everyone. They would all be waiting for me to arrive so they could point and ridicule.

Presently I heard a slight groan, and I knew it was the groan of mortal terror.

That was it. That was the first line. It came to me out of nowhere, or maybe from a small emergency box stuffed away in my crowded brain, a box that contained all the tools I needed to rescue myself. Now, when it mattered, that box opened.

As if all I had needed was a battery jump, I rattled off every line of the story and paused in the correct places for dramatic effect. I slammed my foot into the ground when it was time for the heart to beat; I watched the teacher smile at me in my peripheral vision. When I was done, I could feel my own heart begging to be set free from my chest. It was pounding so hard that I thought everyone else could hear it. I felt sweat beading up on my forehead.

If it were possible for a person to shed their skin and step out as a brand-new entity, I felt like that's what I had done. In that small fraction of time, my consciousness melted and collected around my ankles while the real *me* that had been hidden my whole life was allowed to breathe for the first time. It was like jumping out of a plane without checking your parachute, and somehow trusting fate to save your life. Then, when it was over, I reverted to a wallflower. I didn't thank my audience or notate the end of my performance with any movements or final statements. I just walked back to my desk and sat down.

I don't remember anything after that except standing in the principal's office a few weeks later, waiting for her to get off the phone.

"Well, Mr. Sweeney," she said with a smile. "Looks like you're going to the University of Pennsylvania."

Mr. Sweeney? I'm 11 years old.

I waited for her to elaborate because I had no idea what she was talking about.

"You did really well with your prose from what I heard. Your teacher recorded the audio and submitted it for consideration. The state finals are being held at the University of Pennsylvania."

My stomach sank lower than I thought a stomach could sink.

"And you've been selected!"

Apparently, it was not up to me to decide whether or not I wanted to represent my school. I couldn't decline the invitation or think of an excuse to be absent that day. Or could I? No, I couldn't. This was larger than trying to avoid bullying, though, in some weird way, I was feeling the same kind of push into discomfort as I had when Rick blackmailed me over the forged signature. The underlying culprit was lack of control; I hated the idea of being moved around like a chess piece for the benefit of others.

That fall, I was sitting on a shuttle bus looking out the window at 9 am when everyone else was in school. The bus had been chartered by the school to transport me and two other students to the University. Unbeknownst to me, there were state finals in other academic areas, including Math and Science, and my travel companions were the best in those subjects. My expertise was in English, but somehow, I was also now an authority on Literature.

When the shuttle stopped in front of the University, all I could do was stare blankly through my opaque reflection in the window. The other two students leaped from their seats like contestants on the Price is Right, excited and ready to impress the judges. I slid out of my space as if I was on my way to Guantanamo Bay. We walked through the main entrance and were greeted by a man in a dark blazer whose smile almost wrapped around the back of his head.

"Let me guess," he said. "You're the students from St. Clements."

It must be this patch on my sweater that says St. Clements.

"Follow me."

The inside of the building was massive compared to our small elementary school. I saw a few UPenn students standing around freely without regard for the rules but soon realized there probably weren't any rules once you got to college. Not like there were for us lowly chain-gang kids walking single file because stepping out of line was insubordinate.

The man in the blazer led us into an auditorium that looked like a cross between a Broadway theater and a Catholic church. It was intimidating. The stage rose above the audience and had pipes for sound on either side. Most of the seats were already filled with students close to my age and several adults that were presumably there to judge. We were directed to sit near the front and told that our names would be called when it was time for our respective presentations.

Again, I was there to deliver *The Tell-Tale Heart.* The first line of the segment flooded my head.

...the groan of mortal terror.

Never was "mortal terror" a more appropriate description. I was so anxious that I could feel my body shaking. I could feel my shortness of breath wrestling with the hollow feeling in my stomach. I had somehow gotten through this in front of my class, but now I would be in front of total strangers whose sole purpose was to determine whether or not I was good enough. My school had pushed me into this against my will, and if I bombed, I would go back as a failure and a potential disappointment - all because the teacher noticed me reading books that were inconsistent with my age.

I should've stuck to R.L. Stine.

"Gary Sweeney..."

My name didn't sound like my name. It sounded like the announcer was calling someone else, or maybe calling the physical me while my insides were busy trying to squeeze through the viaducts and escape. I rubbed the palms of my hands against my pants to dry them and stood up, feeling a sea of eyes burning into me as I sidestepped through the aisle and looked up at the stage. It appeared to have doubled in size.

I reached the steps on the right side of the stage and began my ascent, listening to the sound of my dress shoe heels bang against the floor. There was a small podium in the center with a microphone protruding from the top, and my immediate thought was that it wouldn't work for my performance since it was supposed to be, you know, a *performance*. I wasn't delivering a bland speech in the hopes of becoming class president; I was supposed to belt the words of Poe into the air with enough passion to knock the wind out of the room. How could I do that standing in one spot?

I drew a deep breath and stood still for a moment before sliding the podium out of the way. What I was preparing was so out of character that I silently prayed for the strength to get through it.

Ordinarily, I would welcome something to stand behind because it was the same as hiding, avoiding, escapism. But I was so anxious that it turned into anger. I was mad at my teachers for forcing me into a situation that *made me anxious* - sort of a psychological Gordian Knot. And that anger made it possible for me to fight my timidity.

Before I knew it, I was in the middle of my scene, and less than 10 minutes later it was all over. I walked off stage to the sound of light applause and sat down. The man in the blazer smiled and nodded in my direction. The whole thing was very unexceptional, at least outwardly. Inside, my cyclical thought process continued to tear into me with self-deprecation.

They aren't clapping feverishly because you weren't very good. They were only clapping because they had to - because they were being polite. But if they could've gotten away with it, they probably would've booed you out of the room.

The following week my teacher handed me an envelope. Inside was a certificate for "Excellence in Prose" from the University. I was told that certificates were only issued to the top performers - not to the winners - but to the top performers. I put the certificate away somewhere and never looked at it again.

One of the more disheartening side effects of Pop no longer driving was that I couldn't sit in his car on school mornings. By this time, I was old enough to walk myself to the schoolyard but Pop still met me every afternoon as I was coming home, not because he had to, but because he eagerly awaited that 5-minute break in his day. The moment I stepped off the bus, I would see him in the distance wearing his threadbare baseball hat and Etonic-brand sneakers, heading my way with his hands in his pants pockets and a smile plastered across his face. But one day in early December 1990, he wasn't there and I started to panic.

I walked across the concrete parking lot until breaking

into a light jog. I had developed a habit of trying to dodge uncertainty as quickly as possible and needed to find out what was causing Pop's absence, even if it was something traumatic. One of the worst predicaments for someone with anxiety is to *not know* because in those cases, imagination takes over and delivers the worst possible outcome. In my mind, Pop couldn't have simply fallen asleep on the couch longer than planned and missed my arrival as a result; he must have suffered an illness: maybe an aneurysm, or maybe he fell. There were times when Gram would complain about him walking down the basement steps with one of his shoes untied. All it would take is a simple misstep to trip him up and send him hurling to the cold floor thirteen steps down. And then, God only knew what would happen. If he hit his head, that was the end; if he survived the fall and lay unconscious, it might still be the end because Gram didn't drive and all the neighbors who did were at work. How would he get to the hospital? I would race into the house and find Gram screaming for help to an empty room.

The scene repeated on a steady loop as I ran to the corner of their street and saw Pop walking slower than usual, staring at the ground as if lost in thought. I had never seen him like that before.

He's okay.

Pop heard the rustling of my backpack and locked eyes with me. He could tell I needed some kind of explanation; he could also tell I was relieved to see him.

"My brother Billy died," he said.

I didn't know what to say. I had no experience with mourning because no one close to me had ever passed. I also didn't know how close Pop had been to Billy. I knew he took responsibility for placing him with caregivers, but on a personal level, I never knew if they had connected as brothers. There couldn't have been many opportunities for that in their youth.

Billy was always away somewhere, hidden from public view, shrouded.

When Pop and Gram married in 1939, Billy was a 16-year-old living in an asylum amongst other mentally challenged people, some of whom rammed their heads against the wall and screamed or sat in the corner partially clothed. If Billy had ever been visited by his parents, it's unlikely they would have stayed long, just enough to wave hello and give a quick hug; had Pop visited with his new bride, Billy would have been completely unaware that he had a sister-in-law. Those difficulties made it nearly impossible to form a bond, and since learning of Billy, I had only heard Pop speak about him despondently, as someone he pitied, an innocent boy who would never have a normal life.

In the years that followed, a rumor swirled in our family that he had been beaten to death by the people assigned to his care. Like the staff at Pennhurst had done in the 1940s, it would've been easy to abuse Billy without setting off any alarms. And if it was even slightly possible that Billy died at the hands of his attendants, it would mean that Pop led him to it - inadvertently and innocently. But there was never a definitive explanation. As an adult, I took it upon myself to obtain Billy's death certificate, even though I was certain it would never list anything unsavory as his cause of death. Still, what I found suggested serious neglect.

According to his death certificate, Billy suffered a "cerebrovascular accident" (CVA), the medical term for a stroke. Secondarily, he developed an "infected decubitus ulcer," a more technical phrase for bedsore. The major issue was that Billy's bedsores were never addressed or treated, and he likely developed Cellulitis, a life-threatening bacterial skin infection, which turned into Septicemia (listed as his third contributing cause). Finally, he went into cardiopulmonary failure from blood poisoning.

The summer after Billy died, Pop and I went on our last fishing trip. Mike, the adult son of his next-door neighbor, arranged to drive us out to a calm spot in the country and spend the day there. Pop suggested Schwenksville, Pennsylvania so he could return to the Perkiomen Creek he loved so much. We packed a few thermoses and coolers with food and chips to last until dusk, then readied ourselves with insect repellant because I was susceptible to mosquito bites. The drive was about an hour northwest, and on the way, I saw a side of Pop that I never forgot.

Mike struck up a conversation with Pop and it shifted course a few times to cover multiple topics that fed off the one preceding it. They started talking about President Bush and somehow landed on automobile maintenance. I spent that time looking out the window and listening just enough to turn my head and give a quick answer to any question I was asked. Something told me to let Pop have that one-on-one time with another adult since he spent most of his waking life with me, even though he probably would've been just as happy to have me participate.

What I had never heard until that car ride was Pop using profanity. It was mostly gratuitous; there was no real need to punctuate his commentary with expletives aside from the freedom of doing it. Hearing the change in his voice made me look away from the window and listen more carefully, and as usual, I analyzed it.

Much later in my life, I read some work by Alan Watts, a philosopher famous for popularizing Eastern religion in the western world. Watts spoke about a concept that he termed "the element of irreducible rascality," that is, the idea that human beings are a duality of good and bad, and that no one's behavior is absolute because one side cannot exist without the other. He theorized that a rascal is within us at the most primitive level and that its mischievous presence is what makes us human, or the embodiment of imperfection.

Once I understood that belief, I saw Pop as someone more than an important figure in my life. He had become almost ethereal to me but I realized that he was a different person to other people. To Gram, he was a husband; to his daughters, a father. There must have been innumerable coworkers from his past and friends on multiple levels of closeness that knew him as a drinking buddy or the guy they would ask for advice on running a belt sander. So, as he sat in the front seat letting the obscenities fly, he was simply being one of the boys, perhaps the man he used to be on the Midvale shop floor when the radio announcer would feverishly describe a Richie Ashburn homerun.

We arrived at a secluded spot and spread our supplies across the ground. Pop threaded the line through the loops on my fishing pole and then demonstrated the best way to ensure a deep cast across the water. To the left was a short runoff that spilled over and created a beautiful white noise that eliminated the potential for any repetitive sounds I might've heard.

The three of us sat for hours and paid little attention to the poles. Before the day was out, we decided that catching anything was unimportant. The truth was, we didn't much care. The atmosphere, the time, a glide into the painted wilderness which was perfect in the sense that nothing more existed but the air in our lungs and all the colors of heaven - that was what mattered.

As we packed up with the sun falling in the distance, I

took one final shot and lowered a big square net into the river. Five seconds later I pulled up a fish just long enough to snap a photo and released it to its rightful home. Walking back to the car, I had the distinct and unsettling feeling that I would never see Pop with a fishing pole again.

8. SUBMERGENCE

I'll never forget one particularly rainy afternoon when I was sitting at Pop and Gram's kitchen table, and Gram decided to share a family story with me. It was the romantic tale of her parents and it had been circulating among certain relatives for years, but I had yet to hear it. Gram's mother and father were named Archie and Anna Clark, and they were so in love that it transcended death.

Archibald Stewart Clark was born on March 30, 1885, in Philadelphia, Pennsylvania to David Stewart Clark and Letitia Clark. On June 2, 1909, at the age of 24, Archie married his longtime sweetheart, Anna Miller Denis. Anna had just turned 20. The couple took their honeymoon in Atlantic City, New Jersey with a group of friends in tow, and, upon returning to Philadelphia, moved into a small house at 1238 S. 26th Street. Originally a brick-maker by trade, Archie eventually found work as a Gas Maker with the United Gas Improvement Company. Over the next 19 years, Anna gave birth to 9 children (4 boys and 5 girls), beginning with Edward in 1910, and ending with Eleanor in 1928.

Tragedy struck Archie and Anna in 1938, when one of their sons, Archie Jr., died at the age of 17 from a multitude of illnesses, including septicemia, chronic mastoiditis, lateral sinus thrombosis, lung abscesses, and toxic hepatitis. The year prior, Archie Jr. suffered severe burns and smoke inhalation when he was one of two boy scouts trapped in a barn that went up in flames. The fire was attributed to a small oil stove that ignited a bed of dry straw. The sudden loss of their child left a void in the Clark household.

As their other children grew older, married, and moved away, Archie and Anna began to take nightly walks around their neighborhood. For years, they never wavered from their routine of strolling arm-in-arm after dinner. In 1955, the newly dedicated Connell Park opened at 64th & Elmwood Avenue. The Clarks had recently moved to 2142 S. 67th Street and the park's proximity made it easy for Archie and Anna to conduct their evening walks there. Without fail, Archie would ready Anna by saying: "Come on, Annie, let's go for our walk."

Less than a year after Connell Park opened, Archie died on Mother's Day—May 13, 1956. He was 71 years old and had been battling cirrhosis of the liver for three months. Anna was devastated. She remained in her home for a short time before moving to Blackwood, New Jersey to live with her daughter Eleanor.

Two years later in April 1958, Anna saw a familiar face in her sleep. One evening, she dreamt that she was looking through the back window of her Philadelphia home, and saw Archie standing on the outside of their fenced yard. He smiled at her comfortingly, and said: "Come on, Annie, let's go for our walk." Even in the dream, Anna knew that Archie had passed away. Confused, she replied: "I don't

want to go for a walk right now, Archie. I'm too tired."
With that, Archie faded slowly and disappeared.

The following morning, Anna told her children about
the experience. They believed it was random and without
meaning. But the next night, Anna saw Archie for the
second time. Again, she was looking through the window
and noticed Archie standing outside: this time, he was
standing on the inside of the fenced yard. He smiled and
said: "Come on, Annie, let's go for our walk." Anna again
replied that she was too tired and did not want to walk.
Archie disappeared.

Having had the same dream for two successive nights,
Anna was convinced that it had some level of significance.
This thought was solidified when she had the dream
again—for the third night in a row. She was looking
through the window and saw Archie in the middle of the
backyard. Again, he asked her to take a walk, and again she
refused.

The fourth night, Anna dreamt that Archie was no
longer in the yard, but standing at the base of the back
steps. He smiled and looked up at her through the window.
"Come on, Annie, let's go for our walk," he said, but Anna
refused, and Archie vanished.

For the fifth night in a row, Anna went to sleep and
had the same dream. When she woke on the morning of
April 17, she told Eleanor "Your father was at the back
door last night. I was face to face with him. He asked me
to take our walk like he always does."

Later that same day, Anna was rushed to Cooper
Hospital in Camden, New Jersey. Within a few hours, she
passed away from a heart attack.

Theoretically, Anna's next dream about Archie would
have had him entering the house and physically contacting
her. The family believed that Anna had that dream in the

hospital and finally agreed to take a walk with Archie.

The story of Archie and Anna ignited a spark that persuaded me to start documenting the little ancestral histories that were peppered throughout my family tree. I loved the idea of having a captivating lineage because I wanted to believe that something was separating me from everyone else. There were times that I wished I had been related to someone famous or infamous just for the prestige. I did manage to discover that my 4th great uncle, George Crawford Platt (Pop's great uncle), was awarded the Medal of Honor for heroism in the Battle of Gettysburg. In 1979, the Penrose Avenue Bridge, which runs over the Schuykill River in Southwest Philadelphia, was renamed The George C. Platt Memorial Bridge.

When I graduated 8th grade in June 1992, we had a small gathering at my grandmother's house and my father came to see me. The last time he had been in that house, the police were trying to get him out of the bedroom for assaulting my mother. That he was even there suggested a fight had occurred between him and Bernice. For most of the day, he sat quietly in the living room but posed for a few photos with me. We were both wearing a white dress shirt and black pants. The only real memory I have of him from that party is when he left; I walked with him back to his pickup truck (as my mother followed cautiously behind at a respectable distance), said a few words and gave him the kind of uncomfortable hug reserved for uncles you don't know that well. There was no firmness behind his embrace, which to me, suggested guilt, low self-confidence, or a combination of both.

I didn't know it at the time, but that turned out to be the last real interaction I had with my father. Some time later, I tried to call him, but when he answered the phone and heard my voice, he hung up.

That summer, Pop and Gram decided to visit their other daughter in New Jersey and took me along for the week. Although it was just 30 minutes away, it was like stepping into a different world. Most of our family stayed in one area and only a few members lived out of state. Gram loved going to New Jersey because it usually meant an impromptu day trip to Atlantic City whenever the mood struck. She could sit in front of a slot machine longer than a telephone operator sat in front of a switchboard; the flashing lights, ringing bells, and cigarette smoke was her idea of paradise.

Pop was never one for the casino. He much preferred to sit outside and enjoy the sounds of nature. I can't recall a single instance when he was content in a highly active environment. Gram was an extrovert. She loved people, conversations, laughing, and socializing. If she had her way, the doors to their house would have been propped open morning to night so people could walk in and sit down. Pop was her polar opposite. He loved his small circle but was otherwise drawn to peace and quiet.

When we arrived in New Jersey, it was evident that Gram was planning a string of outings. She wanted to shop and take polaroid photos until the evening when she would change into her long, collared nightgown that zipped up the front. And even then, she might have played ten card games before going to bed. For the most part, that meant Pop and I were on our own.

We spent most days just sitting around unless one of my older cousins decided to drag us to the mall. The week was largely uneventful and would've faded into obscurity were it not for one event that was both terrifying and hilarious. After a period of inactivity that was starting to give most of us cabin fever, my great-uncle grabbed the newspaper and scanned through the movie listings. The only movie that everyone could agree upon was some high-tech science-fiction drivel that had no real plot, but that was what *real men* watched. I preferred more complex films because I reveled in the mental acrobatics required to figure out their true meaning. Big action explosions and alpha male rhetoric did nothing for me. It still doesn't.

At the theater, we piled into a row of seats and waited for the previews. When they started, Pop began his loud running commentary to the displeasure of everyone around us. I was amused because it was typical Pop - not rude, just aloof.

The movie was well underway when Pop got up to use the restroom. I was bored out of my mind. Years earlier I had tried to watch *Star Wars* on television and couldn't force myself through it. The lasers and otherworldly fluff were abundant and everyone else my age marveled at the action. And truthfully, I wanted to like it; but to me, it was just a lot of fanfare and bright lights, and I didn't get it. There were too many characters; trying to guess which ones were important and which were space fillers overloaded my senses. In some odd way, I feel like I missed out on the enjoyment I was supposed to have as a kid of my generation.

The movie we were watching wasn't even trying to compensate for a terrible script by distracting us with special effects. It was a two-hour cure for insomnia. I suddenly realized that Pop had never come back from the bathroom and leaned over to my cousin so I could make him aware.

"What do you think is taking him so long?" I whispered.

"He's fine."

A 77-year-old man went to the bathroom and hasn't returned. But, why worry about that?

99

For as unconcerned as my cousin and uncle were, they were a bit edgier when the movie ended over an hour later and Pop was still nowhere to be found. We spilled out into the lobby with the rest of the crowd and started looking around. I went into the men's room and found nothing.

"He's not in there!" I said, frantically.

I ran over to the concession area and tried to describe Pop to the teenagers behind the counter. The confused look on their faces told me that I wouldn't get anywhere with them. My next thought was that Pop had wandered outside for air and gotten lost. We were in a rural part of New Jersey and a few quick turns could easily render someone helpless unless they were highly familiar with the area, which Pop was not.

My uncle looked around the parking lot in vain. Against my better judgment, I walked into the ladies' bathroom, thinking that maybe Pop hadn't bothered to notice the triangular skirt on the wall plate next to the door. But it was another dead end. I couldn't believe what was happening.

How does somebody just disappear?!

We had been out of our movie for over 45 minutes and I felt the suffocation of a panic attack beginning to take hold. My thoughts started to run away from me so quickly that I was breathing in short bursts that sounded like silent hiccups.

He could be in the street. He could've been hit by a car half a mile away from here. We haven't looked that far. He could've walked off in any direction. How do we even know which way to go? We have to call the police. They have a helicopter and can fly over the area. If it gets dark, they have a spotlight.

"Hey, call the police!" I said to my cousin.

As soon as the words came out of my mouth, I heard

the abrupt sound of a door being pushed open and a sudden flood of voices behind it. Crowd murmuring. Random laughter and conversations. Then, a few people parted and I saw Pop walking towards us with a confused look on his face.

"That was the strangest goddamn movie I ever saw in my life!"

The three of us stared at him in disbelief. I glanced up at the theater entrance above his head and noticed that he had just watched the second half of a romantic comedy after watching the first half of an outer space action film. After leaving the bathroom, he walked into the wrong theater and sat down beside three people that he assumed were us. I felt a smile trying to break across my face from the sheer absurdity of it all, but my panic was too strong to let it happen. Instead, the two emotions fought it out on the car ride back to the house.

Although I spent most of my time at Pop and Gram's house at this point, the division in my own home was becoming more obvious. Rick was no longer a threat to me, not because I had outgrown his tyrannical methods (which I had), but because he had fully checked out. He didn't even try to pretend he was invested anymore; he knew my mother was preparing to leave him. The question was *when*.

Part of Rick's obsessiveness was maintaining absolute control over his belongings. His collections became hoards; areas of the house designated for living were now places to store things, and the basement was like his personal apartment. Our basement was split into two parts. The first room was an open square with an indoor-outdoor carpet and a bulbous white General Electric refrigerator that dated to 1945. I used to hold personal Halloween parties there. Because my tastes were atypical and didn't translate well for the kids I considered my friends, I would end up dragging a VCR and a small television down to the room, taping a few cardboard decorations to the wall, and sitting in a plastic chair to watch an old, grainy horror film by myself.

The other part of the basement contained our washer and dryer, and a random assortment of boxes that didn't fit anywhere else. There was a wall-sized sliding closet stuffed with bags and old clothing, and a door to the outside steps that led up to the yard. The closet was Rick's storage unit. Years before, he kept an assortment of baseball card grading magazines in that space, which I didn't understand since the information would be obsolete a month later. But, now that he was all but separated, he had moved his memorabilia and filled the closet with pornographic tapes; I unintentionally discovered them one day while looking for a sheet to hang in front of the basement window so I could make the room darker for one of my solitary movie parties.

My mother never knew the tapes were there until much later. She was deep in the layers of her emancipation plan and had blocked Rick out of her mind. They had been sleeping separately for a while, never ate dinner together, and rarely spoke unless it was quick and in passing. Rick slept on the sofa most nights, which was more or less destroyed because the metal spoke on his belt ripped holes in the pleather material and allowed the stuffing to come through. It looked like someone had driven by and riddled the sofa with machine-gun bullets. The carpet around the sofa was full of stains from spills that he had never addressed, and there were flakes of dead skin from him constantly scratching the psoriasis patches on his arms. As much as it drove me crazy, I had stopped cleaning up after him. It was completely pointless; he could undo three hours of work in five minutes.

The impasse at home pushed me further into isolation. I felt like a tenant sharing a room with two strangers. I was old enough to occupy myself and didn't need help with much, but the constant tension made daily life uncomfortable. Even when it was quiet, it really wasn't. The silence became deafening.

As fall and winter came around, I looked forward to the shorter days. I was always partial to those seasons because there was contentment in the darkness for me. Despite how ominous that sounds, it was more about nighttime quieting the chaos and making it acceptable to wind down. When the sun was out, I felt unspoken pressure to be *doing* something.

With the house in a state of limbo, night meant that the two sides would retire to their corners and I would have silence to process my surroundings. But it wasn't enough for me to lock myself away anymore. I had spent so many years in my room that the walls could no longer provide the level of solitude I craved. In those confines, I was still connected - and I needed distance.

My routine was to wait until roughly midnight when I knew my mother would be asleep with the door closed. Once I was sure she was out, I needed to confirm that Rick was also sleeping, which was trickier since he always kept the television on in the living room so there was no audible way to tell.

The top five steps on our main staircase were obstructed behind a wall. A person descending wouldn't be visible to anyone downstairs until about midway. While this was beneficial in my case, our stairs were also covered with carpet that had thinned from a decade of foot traffic. That meant that the wood underneath made noises and could be heard over the television, and that was *not* beneficial. To remedy this, I would lie on my stomach at the top step and then slide down very slowly, so slowly in fact, that it could take ten minutes before I reached the end of the wall coverage. Once there, I would edge past just enough to see the couch. If Rick was awake, I would reverse the process and wait him out.

When it was safe, I would slink through the living room, nervously watching my large shadow projected on the wall behind Rick as he slept, and open the door leading to the basement. By the time I reached the back room, I had to open the door just as cautiously. Sound traveled in our house like the whole structure was made of cardboard. After unlocking the deadbolt and pushing open the metal screen door on the opposite side, I pulled it closed just enough to look secure. From there, I made my way to the yard and jumped the fence.

I was out. And free.

The first thing I always noticed was the stars. Wintertime is famous for clearing the sky. I would stand there for a few minutes, looking up at those dots of light and wonder about all they had seen. Even more fascinating to me was the idea that every star I could see was from the past, and the old feeling of safety I remembered from the library's history books came rushing back. Because light travels at 186,000 miles per second and the closest star to our Solar System is Proxima Centauri (approximately four lightyears away), it meant that at the very least, any visible star would have begun emanating its light four years earlier, and I was actually seeing it as it would have appeared at the end of the 1980s.

My neighborhood was eerily silent after midnight. All the cars that were so active in daytime sat still as though they were stones in a graveyard. The windows in the houses were black. The number of unconscious people far outweighed those still awake. Nothing stirred, the world was motionless except for the clouds of breath I sent into the cold air like musket fire.

Each time I snuck outside, I took the same route. The rear side of our block was lined with trees. Almost every house had a tree in the patch of grass that ran parallel with the sidewalk. In the summer, this was a great place to stand in the shade; at night, it created a hidden tunnel because the denseness of the clustered trees blocked out the streetlights. I would walk the path to the end and make a left towards Pop and Gram's block. Once there, I would enter the first *breezeway* (a term we used to describe a separation in the rowhomes that acted as a passthrough) in the middle of the block. That divide provided access to the backyards of the homes behind Pop and Gram's.

One house, in particular, had been vacant for years. If you boosted yourself high enough, you could look through the window and see a perfectly-set dining room table, as if the previous owners had prepared to entertain guests who never arrived. It was sort of creepy. However, the back of the house contained a set of three stairs that led to the outside of their basement door. I would always walk down those steps and sit, sometimes for two hours, to think in the quiet darkness. When the cold finally got the best of me, I would walk around the corner and up through our house, stopping to make sure Rick's mouth was still hanging open in slumbrous bliss before heading to my room.

Most often, my mind would continue racing until I watched the sunrise a few hours later outside my bedroom window.

I hadn't known it, but my mother had been fighting my father for child support my whole life. According to the law, he was required to pay support as long as I was in school and living at home. Like most fathers on the wrong end of the legal system, he was usually in default and would have to appear in court several times over the years.

My mother decided to bring me to court with her when I was about 14 years old. I wouldn't be permitted to enter the courtroom; I would have to sit in the waiting area. But the purpose for my attendance, from what I gathered, was so my father could see me in person and, hopefully, feel a level of emotion that would convince him to stop fighting the judge's order and offer the support I needed.

After we arrived, I sat in a stiff, plastic chair at the end of a long hallway. My mother was called into the courtroom despite my father's absence. But no sooner than I shifted into a halfway satisfactory position, I saw the door open on the far side of the room.

My father was 35 but looked double his age. His hair was completely gray, his face was full of wrinkles, there were dark circles under his eyes, and he was walking with a cane. I watched him coming towards me, hobbling, and wondered if he was faking it to garner sympathy. And again, I was projecting what I had been taught to think of him. He would always be dishonest; he would always concoct a scheme; he would never have an attack of conscience.

As he neared me, I locked eyes with him and attempted a smile - something that said "Hi Dad, how are you? I'm doing okay." He briefly looked at me, then shifted his eyes downward, and walked through the courtroom doors without saying a word.

That was the last time I saw him.

9. BROKEN PLACES

Pop began to slow down considerably around the end of 1994. He even stopped walking to the shopping center, which had been one of his favorite pastimes even when there was nothing to buy. As long as I had known him, he had been active, even if that meant tending to the two bushes growing at the top of his front lawn. But I could tell something was catching up to him, maybe the decades of machinery work, or maybe just the general health problems that come with your late 70s.

As it turned out, Pop's increasing weight and disregard for the type of food he consumed, coupled with years of smoking (both cigarettes and cigars) and now lethargy, had pushed him into a different category altogether: danger.

Soon after, he was diagnosed with diabetes and told he would not only need insulin injections every day but regular blood sugar checks. This had larger implications for their household, as Gram could no longer keep a gallon of ultra-sweet iced tea in the refrigerator, nor chocolate cakes and cookies sitting on the counters. If Pop was going to eat candy, it had to be diabetic candy, and he couldn't exactly be trusted to stick with that if there were better-tasting alternatives at arm's reach.

A few days after his diagnosis, a nurse visited the house and spoke with Gram about the proper way to administer shots. She tried to demonstrate on an orange since its peel was the closest texture to human skin, but Gram wasn't paying attention because she had already decided she couldn't handle it. When it came time for her to pierce the orange, Gram turned her head away, closed her eyes, and jammed the needle in like she was playing Pin the Tail on the Donkey. The nurse was visibly frustrated.

Nobody in my family liked needles. I wasn't the biggest fan of watching the sharp, thin point burrow through flesh, but Gram's attempt horrified me. I could tell that Pop was upset about being diabetic, especially because he had prided himself for being fit as a young man and had taken several photos standing in front of his car without a shirt. He once possessed the broad shoulders, narrow waist, and defined biceps prized by women. Coupled with his dark, coiffed hair, he would have been a bonafide star in his small hometown.

Now, he would need medicine and wellness checks for the rest of his life. It was the same fall from grace he had experienced when Midvale closed and rendered him, in his mind, useless.

The nurse suggested other family members who might help.

"Maybe one of your daughters..." she said to Pop.

"I'll do it," I said. "I'm here every day. I can do it."

Pop looked over the top of his glasses at me and I detected a hint of relief on his face. He may not have been convinced that a 15-year-old was the best choice, but it was clear that Gram was out and no one else was around frequently enough to take responsibility. The only other alternative was to pay a nurse daily and that was unrealistic.

Although she looked skeptical, the nurse consented, but not before asking me a million times if I was certain. There was no way I would abandon Pop; that was all the certainty I needed.

First, there was the issue of drawing the insulin into the needle. I had to be very careful not to allow bubbles. The nurse gave me a laundry list of negative effects that would have, which, with my anxiety, felt the same as positioning me in front of a firing squad wearing a blindfold. Of equal importance was making sure I rotated the injections each day. Pop could never get his shot in the same location two days in a row. If I started with his right arm, the following day would be his left arm, then left leg, and finally right leg - clockwise from my vantage point.

The day we began, Pop was sitting on the edge of his bed wearing a black tank top. I was nervous but trying to keep it together. When I had been forced to read Poe in front of strangers, I could've actually walked off the stage. I wouldn't have gotten detention or been reprimanded. Nothing would've happened aside from a bit of embarrassment. But this was pressure from a new angle. There was no stage to vacate.

I prepared the needle with the correct amount of insulin and triple-checked that all the bubbles were gone. Then, I wiped a small area with rubbing alcohol, took a deep breath, and pushed the needle into his arm. He never flinched.

"Done already?" he asked.

I nodded with a half-smile, still feeling my stomach in the throes of a gymnastics routine. I pulled the needle out slowly, gave another quick dab with the alcohol pad, and covered it with a Band-Aid. From that point on, I was less nervous because Pop was at ease. Knowing that he trusted me with something as important as giving him insulin, in some way, boosted my confidence.

As much as I could, I stopped him from grabbing the wrong iced tea when he wanted a drink and hid any visible sweets before he saw them. I checked his blood sugar every day and kept a log of his readings in an old school notebook that once served as my scratchpad for doodles and short stories.

Every so often, the nurse would stop by as a courtesy and I would sit with her to go over Pop's numbers. Mainly, I wanted to know if there was more I could do. I was able to give the shots on autopilot, but aside from the bit of knowledge I had on what to avoid, I felt like I was maintaining Pop rather than improving him.

Unfortunately, maintenance was the only thing left.

Pop couldn't exercise to lose weight because he was always tired. When he would go up or down the steps, it was one stair at a time and a short breath in between. It hurt me to watch those changes materialize in him. I still remembered the vibrant Pop who could walk blocks in Philadelphia humidity just to grab a non-essential item because he had nothing better to do. The traces of that man were still present in his eyes, but his body had let go rather abruptly. In just a few short years, he had gone from self-sufficiency to complete dependence.

Over the next year, I became Pop's full-time caretaker when I wasn't in school. One of the most challenging tasks was giving him a bath.

Pop and Gram didn't have a shower. They had an old, monstrous clawfoot tub that could've doubled as a warship. It became very slippery with the smallest touch of water and that was too disastrous to think about, especially because the bathroom was very small and full of sharp edges. Instead, I convinced Pop to let me help him. I would sit him down to remove his shoes, socks, and pants. Then, I would pull him to a standing position and tell him to hold onto the sink as I lifted off his shirt. I made sure he saw me turning away while he stepped out of his underwear so I could spare him the indignity. I held his arm and watched him place one foot into the water, then the other, and carefully guided him to the tub floor. He was at his most vulnerable - ironically, the way I had been so many times in my youth when all I wanted to do was disappear. And at those times, Pop had been there for me. I never heard a single word of judgment come out of his mouth; he was able to sense when I was overloaded and did what he could to remove me from the line of fire.

Sometimes, that was as simple as a pat on the shoulder and the freedom to pick my favorite candy. Other times, it was listening to his teenage stories about life in the 30s and the thousands of nature sounds he could hear in the summer as he would lie on the grass watching the clouds float by. Regardless of how Pop chose to run interference, it always stopped my anxiety, and my adolescence was held together by surviving for those small, powerful moments.

By the time Pop needed my help to bathe and manage his diabetes, I was starting my junior year in high school. My days were so scripted that I could have navigated with my eyes closed. I would drop my book bag against the inside wall of Pop and Gram's living room at the end of the day and walk straight to the kitchen so I could pull the sugar test strips from the cabinet. Then, I would ask Pop what he ate and look at Gram for non-verbal confirmation. Most times she would nod her head without looking up from her magazine.

Depending on where Pop needed his insulin, we would either stay at the table or go to the sofa so he could roll up his pant leg. Whenever it was a leg injection and we were out of earshot, Pop would rattle off a joke, sometimes two or three, while I was getting the needle ready.

"Hey, so one guy says to the other guy: 'Did you hear about the gent who was hit by the train? The train hit him right in the ass!'"

"Then the other guy says: 'Don't you mean rectum?'"

"Rectum? It didn't wreck 'em, it killed 'em!"

Without fail, Pop would laugh and I would smile. It was likely that he had already told me the joke, but I wouldn't make it obvious.

Because I wasn't far from turning 16, I began taking driving lessons from an older man named Mr. Dunbar. He had been a driving instructor for so many years that he was unafraid of getting into an accident, at least it seemed that way. Once a week, he took me out in his own car, which was specially fitted with a set of breaks on the passenger side.

Part of me felt guilty for preparing to drive since I knew how much Pop wanted his license back, but I reasoned that I could take him places once I was behind the wheel. We practiced correct signaling and lane changing; I mastered parallel parking and knew the meaning of every road sign I could possibly encounter. But then came the study booklet for the written part of the test and my mind went blank. Over and over, I tried to read it but nothing would stick. Although I wanted my license desperately, the information in the dull, off-white pages and the dated clip art rendered my brain unresponsive. Nothing about it interested me.

Shakespearean wording? Not a problem.

Complex sociological debates? Wonderful.

A discussion on the physics of time travel? Yes, please.

Is a man crossing the street while tapping a cane blind

or does he have a disability? That simply didn't compute. Both should've been correct. Instead of memorizing the answers in the booklet, all I could do was decide how much of it made no sense.

I failed the written test twice and then passed by the slimmest margin known to man. I scored perfectly on my driving test.

Once I was a licensed driver, my mother gave me her Dodge Shadow and bought a new car. I found excuses to drive anywhere and everywhere, as any 16-year-old would; though, it was less about exercising new independence than being able to take Pop out. If I had to pick up something for school, he came along; when he and Gram needed to do food shopping, we drove to a grocery store a bit further away to maximize our car time. The more we drove around, it became clear that he was starting to lose control of his bladder. I began placing a towel on the car seat before picking him up, and fortunately he never noticed it. I always had an explanation planned just in case.

Two months later in March 1995, Pop turned 80 years old. We decided to throw a surprise party at the Mantua Masonic Lodge in New Jersey, where Pop would be greeted by not only his entire family but countless old friends, some of whom had been part of his life since the 1930s. We implored Gram to keep it a secret, which was like asking the wind not to blow. Surprisingly, she managed to keep a lid on it. We began setting up a buffet lunch and bought a square cake that could accommodate about 75 people.

Four days after Pop's birthday, we held the party and everyone waited for his grand entrance. He thought he was attending some random affair that required a jacket and tie, so he spruced himself up and left the house with Gram and their daughter Nancy. When they started to walk through the door of the lodge and the guests braced themselves to surprise him, Gram walked in first and received the big applause. Pop wandered in a few seconds later, still unaware of what was happening.

A family friend videotaped the party and captured well wishes from most everyone in attendance. But the real gem of the afternoon was one special present that I couldn't wait for Pop to open. I had suggested it a few months prior and we spent that time searching for places in the area that carried such items. When it finally came time for presents, I stood beside Pop and collected the cards after he finished reading them. Then, we slid an oblong box in front of him and I stood back to watch his expression. He peeled through the layers of paper and dropped them on the floor. I could feel my anxiety rising but it wasn't from fear; it was pure anticipation because I was certain that my prediction for Pop's reaction was correct.

He reached the box, opened the lid, and beamed as I had never seen before.

"Hey! A mandolin!"

The rest of the day was a blur of people laughing and walking around with paper plates while Pop sat and tuned his instrument, lowering his ear closer to the strings so he could hear over the noise in the room. I watched him from the opposite side of the table, knowing that in his personal silence, he was going back to the world he had known as a teenager. The mandolin was more than a nice gesture on our part; it was a voucher for a train ride into yesterday, where the young man he was harboring in his soul could finally take off his old jacket and crack his knuckles.

10. NINETEEN NINETY-SIX

On January 6, 1996, Philadelphia was hit with the largest snowstorm in its history. I was a senior in high school, and not unaccustomed to taking public transportation in harsh weather. Our school was set up to work in tandem with the city's bus system. On days when the charter was late, we could easily hop on a different route, grab a connecting train midway, and still make it to class on time. But this storm was different. In the course of two days, 30.7 inches fell on the area. Then-Mayor Ed Rendell declared a state of emergency, schools shut down, and everything went dark.

Because of narrow streets and limited resources, the Department of Transportation rarely plowed when it snowed, even in smaller storms. This time, clearing paths was out of the question. The neighborhoods were so deeply engulfed that it was impossible for a work truck to navigate; furthermore, if plowing had been possible, it would have buried the cars already trapped in their parking spots. The news stations couldn't even estimate when schools would reopen. Some kids used the time to form their own shoveling militias and spent hours working from house to house (a good day could easily net close to $100). Others enjoyed the long break, traipsing through the alleys and around to adjacent blocks to survey the landscape. Many neighbors banded together to start digging themselves out.

By the time January 8th came, everyone felt like they had run a marathon. Something as simple as walking to the corner required the strength of several people. The snow was still waist-high, and moving meant having to pull your legs up to your chest with each step. I had been outside most of the day with friends and was nearing the end of my stamina. It was barely dusk; I could see the sun disappearing behind the post office, where we spent endless hours finding old tennis balls on the roof and trying to point out landmarks in the next town on clear afternoons.

Before long, I heard a faint noise in the distance, mostly inaudible but strong enough to identify as Gram's voice, straining like something urgent was happening. I couldn't have been more than two streets away, but trying to rush back was pointless with the many white trenches between me and the house. I started back in her direction, thinking at most that she needed a few items from the store; but, after several minutes, I realized she was screaming my name at the top of her lungs. Suddenly my anxiety came through the pit of my stomach and knocked the wind out of me. I knew that there was a problem because although it wasn't unusual for her to poke her head from behind the screen door and yell out, she would always quit after a few attempts when it was obvious I wasn't in range. But she wasn't stopping; she was becoming more frantic.

To this day, I can hear the sound of her calling me.

I remember glancing up at the street lights and seeing their muted glow against the half-darkened sky, and hearing nothing else as if the world had settled down in a grand theater to await the start of some tragic play. There was a heaviness in my ears, a vibration, overpowering the mess of imagery passing across my field of vision. I forced myself to walk faster, and faster until I reached the corner of the block and heard a rise in Gram's urgency. She was holding the top of her shirt closed to ward off the night air, repeating my name in a fit of delirium as a few worried onlookers stood nearby.

By the time I reached the house, she had gone back inside. I looked at a neighbor holding watch by the front door. "You better get in there," she said in a voice that came through like warped vinyl. "Your grandfather is sick."

Two at a time, I bolted up the outside steps and tore into the living room, where I heard a maddened chorus of people trying to make sense of what was happening. I froze when I saw Pop slumped in his dining room chair, his head angled backward at 90 degrees with an empty gaze fixed on the ceiling, gasping for breath like his lungs had suddenly filled with wet cement. I felt paralyzed as if everything surrounding me had been pulled up into a windstorm. The movements before me were fluid and slow until Gram turned with her eyes ripped wide open and broke through the many levels of denial protecting me from trauma.

"Gary, help!"

My first thought was to talk to him. Somehow, I thought he would understand. I made my way over and touched his wrist, feeling the cold metal of his Timex watch in my palm.

"Pop!"

Nothing. He kept wheezing heavily. I knew he couldn't breathe. He couldn't breathe and I was powerless. His familiar brown-framed glasses began to slide lower on his face from the severity of his convulsions. I tried again to get his attention.

"Pop, it's me! Look, look at me, Pop. It's Gary. Pop, right here!"

He turned his head slightly and his eyes locked with mine. But there was emptiness. No recognition. It was like he was staring at a blank canvas. I ran through our many adventures: the candy store across from Patterson, fishing, breakfast in the warmth of his car during the winter, the *Dukes of Hazzard*. Each one flashed in light and smoke like I had conjured a photographer to recreate the happiest moments of my life, one more time. And then, I came back to reality, where Pop was suffocating again, where he was at his most vulnerable. This giant of a man who always knew how to pull me out of myself was now out of my reach. He could not speak to me, but even if he had been able to muster one or two words, I knew he would have been talking to a stranger.

After what felt like an hour, a nurse arrived and told us to move Pop to the living room floor. Four of us lifted him out of his chair and carried him under the iron-framed doorway leading into the next room before lowering him onto the carpet. I vaguely remember someone calling an ambulance. The only thing that made sense to me was loosening his shirt. I fumbled around with the buttons, trying to stop my hands from shaking so I could provide some kind of relief. His breathing was getting worse.

I was eventually pushed out of the way. The nurse did her best to practice whatever training she had received as I paced around in a square, waiting for the smallest indication that everything was going to return to normal.

By the time the paramedics showed up, it was dark. The road conditions were so treacherous, and the drifts of snow so dense, that the closest the ambulance could park was five long blocks away. I saw one of the men unraveling what looked like a small tent. When he pulled it across the floor, I noticed it was a portable stretcher. He started pointing in different directions, giving orders, but I didn't hear anything. Gram barely waited for the fire to burn out of her cigarette as she smashed it into her ashtray and lit another, causing a permanent cloud of smoke to circle our frenetic bodies.

One - two - THREE!

Pop was shifted onto the cloth stretcher and fastened down with several straps. The paramedics made preparations to get him past the front door, through the indoor porch area, and into the night. I ran ahead when I remembered that there was still a pile of snow waiting outside, and started furiously kicking it away to clear a path. By then, it seemed like everyone in the neighborhood was gathered in a small group on the sidewalk; I could tell they wanted an update, but I had no answers to give them. We didn't even know what was happening. I heard the screen door open behind me and spun around to see four men carrying Pop. They continued until they reached the middle of the street. Then, they put him down.

"We'll have to drag him," one of them said.

My throat tightened.

"Drag him?! He's 80 years old!"

"The snow is too deep and the ambulance is too far. If we want to get him there as fast as possible, we need to drag him along the ground."

I started to protest but was cut off mid-sentence.

"We don't want to; we *have* to. But don't worry. This stretcher works like a sled."

One of the paramedics pulled a strap from beneath the stretcher, wrapped it around his wrist, and began pulling as hard as he could while trying not to slip on the coat of ice forming in the dropping temperature. I ran alongside, watching Pop and continually bending down mid-stride to brush away the snow that kept gathering between his face and the inside of the canvas. It was already freezing and I could hear his gasping over the sound of our feet plunging into the white storm. As we continued on, the unsteady footing beat us into exhaustion. My legs were burning, my eyes were watering from running against the cold air, and I shivered uncontrollably. The head paramedic slowed, and without thinking, I grabbed the strap from his hand and began to pull the stretcher myself. Almost every window on the street filled with concerned faces and covered mouths. Random voices bounced off the houses as I struggled to get Pop closer to the end of the block.

What's happening to Bruce?! Is he okay?!

I couldn't tell who was asking, but I said nothing. I didn't have enough strength to look around; I barely had enough strength to walk. But there were several blocks to go and the other paramedics had gone off to ready the ambulance. The strap from the stretcher cut into my hand as I rounded the corner and pulled with a sudden burst of energy. I looked back at Pop and saw him grabbing at his chest.

Was he having a heart attack? Was that causing him to struggle?

I never forgot the first time I heard someone describe the feeling of a heart attack - "like a tank was sitting on their chest." When I saw the way Pop was motioning, I thought for sure he was in cardiac arrest. That would also explain why he couldn't speak to me when I tried to get his attention. He was too short of breath. That had to be it.

In the distance, I could see the red lights of the ambulance flashing across the trees in the park. I could see the exhaust billowing up through the branches and the light emanating from the opened rear doors. The end was in sight, but the remaining distance was uphill. Pop was still sucking in small pockets of air every few seconds; each time he wheezed, I pulled harder. Finally, one of the paramedics standing by the ambulance ran back to meet me and took him the rest of the way. I followed closely behind and tried to help them load him into the ambulance but was held back.

"We got it."

"Do you know what's happening?" I asked. "Is it a heart attack? It seems like a heart attack."

"We don't know yet. The doctors will know."

The only thing I could see was tubes, machines, packets being ripped open, medications, whiteness, chaos, and Pop, now a helpless old man in crisis, flat on his back with a million question marks looming before him. The doors of the ambulance were closed with a sharp thud that sounded like two gunshots, and the sirens came on full blast. As it pulled away, I sat on my knees in the snow and watched it disappear into uncertainty.

Once I arrived back at the house, everyone was trying to figure out how to get to the hospital. We knew Pop was being taken to Fitzgerald Mercy, but we also knew that the roads were still unsafe for a regular car. We calculated possibilities long into the night before finally admitting we wouldn't make it to the ICU until the following day.

The next thing I recall is being in a private space with a doctor and other family members. It was set up like a conference room, presumably where bad news was delivered, amidst soft pastel colors, decorative plants, and calming paintings on the walls. There was also an end table with a box of tissues, and I knew why that was there. Without fail, someone would always cry. Whenever the proverbial rug of hope was pulled from beneath a patient's loved ones, the moment their optimism was forced to kneel before darkness, there would be at least one person whose stone facade would crash into their throat. I looked around and wondered which one of us it would be.

The doctor sat us down and exhaled.

"He had a massive stroke on the left side of his brain, which controls memory, speech, and language. The damage was severe and instantaneous."

When I had been talking to Pop in his chair the night before, calling his name, begging for an indication that he was aware, his brain had already pushed me into a vacuum with everyone else he once loved. The doctor told us, in no uncertain terms, that Pop would never recover. If by some twist of fate he woke up, he would never recognize any of us again.

I heard crying; one of us had cracked but I couldn't identify the voice from my state of suspended consciousness. I wandered out of the room and through the hallway, past other rooms and other families, with a blank stare on my face and ringing in my ears. I didn't quite believe the news; something about it wasn't real.

Pop was immortal to me. He was too important, too much of a constant, almost of another makeup entirely. He couldn't just...*die.* The doctors had to be wrong. Despite Pop's age, poor overall health, and inactivity, there had to be some recourse that would veer us toward a better prognosis. I refused to accept the idea that we had no options, that scientific advancements in the 20th century had not come far enough to rewire Pop's brain and undo the deficits caused by his stroke. Magic Johnson had announced in 1991 that he was HIV-positive and that was as good as a death sentence. And yet, he was somehow thriving against all odds. I wanted to know *why* we couldn't expect the same kind of miracle.

For the next week, we lived in the hospital. Even with a clearly defined visitor policy, there was rarely a moment when Pop was alone. I arrived every morning, early, and sat next to his bed talking as though he was beside me on his living room sofa. In response I heard the sound of his breathing machine, but nothing more. The team of nurses who had been assigned to him would never say whether or not they thought Pop could hear us.

Throughout the day, we would have to remind ourselves to eat. None of us wanted to leave unless it was unavoidable, so we ate downstairs in the cafeteria, which even under happy circumstances (like celebrating a birth) would have been unpalatable. I picked at french fries more often than I ate them, sometimes arranging them into small structures and other times carving lines into the styrofoam plate as if I was counting down to the end of my prison sentence. Pop had slipped into a coma by the time he was admitted and showed no signs of coming out. It didn't stop me from wishing and hoping, but somewhere in the most cluttered recesses of my mind, I knew we were slowing to an eventual stop.

On the evening of Sunday, January 14th, our family was gathered at Pop's bedside, each spending a few moments talking with him about some of his favorite things. I don't remember what I said to him, but knowing the bond we had, I can only assume it was a recap of an old *Sanford and Son* rerun or the latest antics of Archie Bunker. Whenever either of those shows was on television, Pop would lean back into the couch cushion, lock his fingers behind his head, and laugh out loud. It was great to see him that happy, so I would often scan through the listings and try to plan the afternoon around those half-hour segments. After Pop stopped driving and I began taking him places, I made sure that we were never out during one of his shows. He wouldn't have cared about missing any of them, but I cared about the small joys he got, anytime he got them.

My grandmother leaned closer to talk with him, and at the end of her conversation, she said "Dad, if you want to go, it's okay. We understand. You can go if you want. Don't stay just because of us."

At 6:00 a.m. the following morning, I was asleep on my grandmother's sofa until the phone woke me. Through blurry eyes, I saw her pick up the receiver; everything she said was in hushed one- and two-word responses. After a few moments, she hung up the phone, composed herself, and looked over at me.

Pop was gone.

He had survived exactly one week. The doctors later told us that for anyone to hang on that long after such a debilitating event was rare and showed a tremendous amount of strength. It wasn't much consolation, but it reinforced a belief that he hadn't died immediately because he was waiting; and when he knew it was time to let go, he did.

I could never process anything without a deep exploration into the cause and ultimately, an interpretation of what it really meant. Something as complex as death was so daunting that I wasn't sure I would ever be fully satisfied with whatever I found. But I never believed that we were only flesh; I believed in a soul, an essence, something beyond human understanding that comprised us. The body is like a house, a tangible presence to make us recognizable in a concrete world; but within those walls lies our being, and when that untamable force has decided that it no longer wishes to be restrained, the house begins to deteriorate in preparation for an exit.

Turn off the lights.
Draw the curtains.
Lock the doors.
Sleep.

11. WINTER

Our memory is composed of small, individual pieces that have no relevance until they join together to form a complete picture, and that picture is stored somewhere in our subconscious. From the moment a memory is tucked away, we start finding triggers in minutiae: a familiar smell, a song, or a turn of phrase that brings it back to life. And suddenly, what used to be gone is new again.

The first few nights after Pop's death, I continued to stay with my grandmother. I couldn't bring myself to enter Pop and Gram's house where traces of his life still remained in every corner, shrouded with the weight of his absence. It was too much to reconcile emotionally. Yet, it made sense to me on some level: we're born and we die. What matters is the time between those two points and the impact we leave on those around us. I tried to force logic over my sentimentality; if I could analyze the end of Pop's life from a philosophical standpoint, I would accept it as part of his total being. Maybe the Akashic Records really existed - and his soul, like every other soul throughout history and in the future, would be imprinted somewhere in the universe on a different plane of consciousness. And so, his would not be a death, nor would there be such finality, except to those still tangled in their own humanness.

When I think back on it now, I was just trying to stop myself from falling apart. Being my first personal experience with loss and the worst introduction I could have possibly had, I was facing a level of emptiness that I believed was insurmountable.

Sleeping was impossible so I would lie awake, watching the red digital numbers on the bedside clock change until a sliver of dawn crept through the side window. Then, I would get out of bed and walk downstairs on autopilot.

Pop's funeral was held on January 18th, two days before my 17th birthday. Oddly, the night leading up to it, I fell into a deep sleep almost as soon as I hit the pillow. To this day, I remember the dream I had with perfect clarity:

I found myself standing on the block where Pop and Gram lived, though it looked different and I could not see the end of it. The sidewalk stretched far out into the horizon until it disappeared. Every house on the block was identical and there seemed to be hundreds, if not thousands, of them; they were extremely tall and white with an indistinct façade. None of the houses had an address or any defining characteristics. I remember thinking that they looked like unpainted resin models.

Because I knew that I was on Pop and Gram's street, I began to look for their house. I walked until I came to the spot where I thought it should be, but when I tried to look through the front window, something was obstructing my view. It wasn't anything physical; it was more of a dark glare, similar to tint. I tried to approach the door but my legs would not turn. So, I continued to walk straight. After some time, I realized that I had walked miles, and the large white houses continued to appear the further I went.

Eventually, I came upon a friend of mine from the neighborhood, who seemed unfazed by the surroundings, and I asked him to explain what was happening.

"These are our new homes," he told me.

"New homes? But they're all the same," I replied. He nodded and smiled. I looked again at the houses and turned back to him.

"How are we supposed to know which house belongs to us?"

"Well, they're arranged alphabetically," he said. "I've already seen mine."

"Have you seen mine?"

"Yes. I can take you to it."

We started walking. He was ahead of me and the distance between us felt like it was expanding so I hurried to keep up. The ground beneath me was hazy and the houses were passing in a blur like a carousel moving too fast. Until he stopped and pointed.

"There. That's your house."

I turned to my left to find a tall, plain-looking structure that would have been just as enigmatic as the others were it not for one small difference: I could see through the front window.

Pop was sitting in his old familiar dining room chair with his back turned to me. I walked toward the house, keeping my eye on him through the window. The second I walked through the door, he stood straight up and pushed the chair backward. I was still. Then, he turned around and gave me a beaming smile before stretching his arms out to invite me towards him. He looked just as I remembered him: the same thick white hair, the same mannerisms, but with no hints of illness or worry.

There was an immediate feeling of safety as soon as he hugged me.

"I'm okay," he said. "I'm with my parents and Billy."

I woke up with a combination of relief and dread. There was some kind of message from Pop swirling around in my brain that convinced me he was at peace. But in the real world - *my* world - it was morning, and that meant I had to walk into a room and stare at his lifeless body.

In a full-length mirror, I saw my reflection button up a white shirt and step into a pair of black pants. I had learned how to knot a tie by watching Rick during his pre-work ritual. His obsessive tendencies compelled him to undo and redo the process several times before he was satisfied, so it was like having the benefit of rewinding a live person. Without much emotion, I finished readying myself and dropped into the cushion of my grandmother's sofa.

The family would arrive a half-hour before the viewing officially began to release their most painful cries, and then people would filter in and out, express their condolences, put their arms around us, say a prayer for Pop by the edge of his casket, and walk away.

That's all there was for them to do.

It took 80 years for Pop to live his life - 80 years of trials, good times, and heartbreak - 80 years full of experiences, friendships, challenges, feelings, days, nights, children, love, and depression - and yet those who knew him could say goodbye, forever, in less than three minutes. The unfairness of this ran through my mind on a continuous loop until it was interrupted by the sound of my grandmother's front door opening, signaling that it was time to leave.

Pop was handled by Kish Funeral Home on 65th &

Elmwood Avenue, two blocks from where I had attended my first viewing seven years earlier when a neighbor was robbed at gunpoint and murdered for his bus pass and the $5 bill in his wallet. It was still snowing as we pulled into the parking lot; we walked in unison through the double doors and into the foyer, where I felt the first of many lumps in my throat. One room away, Pop was silent. The undertaker greeted us with the usual cordialities and did his best to prepare us for the inevitable. Though I wanted to avoid the viewing room, I also wanted everything to end, and it couldn't end until it began. Anxiety took hold of my insides as I cautiously moved my eyes towards Pop's casket - just enough to see floral arrangements with sashes that read "Husband," "Father," "Grandfather," and "Friend."

As I stepped under the next doorway, the family members surrounding me faded away and my peripheral vision dulled until there was nothing on either side but low lighting. My legs felt heavy when I tried to move them. Thick drapes hung on all sides of the room and the aroma of the flowers was overbearing. I darted my eyes rapidly, trying to absorb the sensory nightmare, not realizing I had been clutching a laminated prayer card in my hand so tightly that it was almost bent in half. On the front of the card was a scenic photo of the mountains with a blue sky in the background - fitting since Pop loved nature; on the back, the words *In Loving Memory, Wilbur B. Edwards, March 22, 1915 - January 15, 1996*, followed by *Footprints*, renowned prose about a man walking along the beach with God.

I bit the inside of my cheek and felt my stomach turn, staring at the floor and tracing the carpet patterns around in circles the same way I had followed the makeshift constellations on my bedroom ceiling as a child. When I finally looked up and saw Pop lying there in his dark suit, with his hair neatly parted and his hands calmly placed just above his waist, the part of me that once felt secure in his presence suddenly cracked and broke into embers.

Ridden with guilt for my apprehension, I walked to the edge of the casket and my anxiety forced me to dig my fingers into the plush, white lining. When I looked at his face, I knew he wasn't there. His body was in front of me, but he wasn't there. What remained was the physical, weathered container that he had outgrown. I told myself that the person I knew had found some other place to go, and maybe, it was like climbing through a window and escaping across a field toward the warm sun.

When I thought about his selflessness over the years, I realized that if Heaven existed, if there was a world with no suffering, he deserved to be there. And at that moment, I needed to believe in something else, something greater without a human explanation and independent of our theories on space and time. I needed to know that he was traveling, moving, continuing onto an endlessness that I, with my temporal limitations, could not detect, but which nonetheless was there. Maybe, like the wind, he would always be felt, even though he could not be seen.

When I backed away from Pop's remains, a sea of muffled voices began to fill the room and I realized that most of the neighborhood had congregated behind me, not wanting to intrude on what appeared to be my last moment of privacy with him.

Pop always told me that he was "tired of living and scared of dying." Despite the obvious assumption that he was quoting lyrics from *Ol' Man River*, there was a revelation in those words and I began to understand what he meant as I sat down and watched the visitors file past, some pausing to touch his hand, others never breaking stride.

I don't think he was afraid of *death* as much as he was afraid of *dying* because dying was a process; his funeral, with glassy-eyed people moving like a band of mannequins, was part of that process - a single act in a complete production - like the graveside prayer and the sympathy cards that would fill our collective mailboxes for weeks to come. Long after he had transitioned out of this world, the ripple effect of his passing would continue to hurt the ones he cared about.

For most of the service, I quietly stared like a person in shock. Part of me wanted to get up and run as far as my legs would take me, but the greater part of me wanted to fall asleep and wake up to the knowledge that all of it had been a mind game. I had heard about rare occurrences where people disassociate from reality and experience a series of events that appear to be real, only to find they weren't upon returning to themselves. For a split second, I actually considered that I might have conjured everything from the snowstorm and Pop's stroke to the weeklong hospital visits out of thin air, which meant I was also now attending a nonexistent funeral.

When the final group of people nodded their heads in our direction, pursing their lips in that familiar expression of pity, we readied ourselves for a slow drive to Arlington Cemetery in Drexel Hill.

I lined up as a pallbearer.

My mind flashed back to *Footprints* on Pop's funeral card and the irony of him being carried when his body could no longer continue. Holding the casket arm and helping to march him through the graveyard to a spot of eternal rest was the last thing I could do for him. I would be there to walk him away from a world that had been unfair, a world that included Midvale and all the people who hadn't cared enough to help, a world that allowed him to age and deteriorate just enough to still be cognizant of the youthful man he was leaving behind. I was showing up to take him home like he had done for me over a decade before, when I would nervously scratch into the faded carpeting at Patterson until I saw him come through the door on his invisible white horse.

I remember sliding the casket into the back of a hearse and then sitting in the backseat of a black car. At the cemetery, a procession of mourners pulled behind us and I looked through the first few rows of headstones at a pile of dirt covered with a green blanket.

Everything ends.

For some reason, that phrase kept repeating in my head when I saw Pop's burial spot.

Everything ends.

Everything ends.

I had been having my cemetery dream for years, and whenever I saw the engraved names, it always made me wonder who those people had been in life. I had a strange fascination with inventing histories for those who had been dead a long time. As soon as Pop's casket was moved from the hearse and my hand was wrapped around the handle, we moved carefully toward the prepared space and I glanced down at the stones we were passing.

Elizabeth Stewart
1847-1910

Elizabeth hadn't been that old. But, by the standards of 1910, living to the age of 63 wasn't bad. She had presumably lived somewhere nearby at the time of her passing, and there were no other "Stewart" burials around her. Had she been a spinster? A married woman whose husband was unfaithful, causing her to revert to her maiden name and declare her strong womanhood once more in death by sleeping alone forever?

I would never have answers, but the lack of anything definitive left all of the doors open in my mind. The cemetery must have been full of stories. Someday, I told myself, I could write a book about these people.

We reached Pop's grave and lowered him onto a set of straps that were draped across the opening in the ground. A pastor stood by with an open bible, waiting to read a passage that would provide the comfort of knowing that Pop was in a better place. I had been to enough masses in Catholic school to understand the process. We needed to trust God's plan, even though we didn't have the capacity to rationalize it. Despite the pain we were feeling, we had to accept that God's time is different than our time and that Pop was taken because he was called elsewhere. Whatever his purpose had been on Earth, that journey was over.

I stood there and stoically ruminated on the predestined ending point we all have from the moment we take our first breath. Maybe we exist in the series of circumstances that occur between the two, and the years move along a curve until the loop closes and we become a full circle. Maybe our bodies were designed to carry our souls through this mortal realm until we find the way out, and then we're free to go.

Those of us left behind to suffer the loss of our loved ones are not afforded the privilege of knowing when that time will be, so we have to watch them leave without the ability to see it coming. At least that's how it is in most cases.

The pastor delivered his quick sermon but I didn't hear anything he said. I slipped into one of my sensory hallucinations and began obsessing over the focal points before me. My eyes glazed over and I felt like I was somewhere else.

I'm not here, am I? I'm definitely not here. I'm not really standing on this grass. Those muffled voices in the distance are fading and will soon be pulled back into a vortex to disappear. Then it will be obvious that I'm not here. I'm staring at this place from the inside of another window. All of these people are apparitions. I'm not here.

And then, it stopped.

I was in reality again and people were starting to drift back to their cars. The funeral was over. Two men stood on either side of Pop's grave with shovels, waiting for us to leave so they could finish their morning assignment.

Their morning assignment. That's all that Pop was to them - a job number, a box they needed to check, nobody important. From my position, I could see cars moving along the road outside the cemetery fence. Others sat in fast food drive-thrus waiting for their lunch. The day was like any other to the rest of the world, fully engulfed in their routines without the slightest indication that someone like Pop was gone.

How do they not know? How can they just carry on as if nothing has changed?

"Come on, Gary," I heard someone say.

All I could think about was Gram having to return to that empty house. She and Pop had been married for 57 years and now she had to sleep in their bed for the rest of her life without him. She had to get up in the morning and make coffee for herself, and no one else. She had to cook breakfast, lunch, and dinner for one, not two. Of course, our family would come together and those small glimpses of normalcy would stay her feelings of loneliness, but when everyone went home and the ticking of her kitchen clock echoed in the new silence, that would be a weight none of us could lift.

Like all funerals I had attended, the service was capped with a lunch gathering as a way of celebrating the deceased. We filtered into the restaurant with our dark clothing and reddened eyes and tried to focus on the good times, while we ate. It was hard to think about food or anything associated with the living. The idea of enjoying something that Pop could no longer have ripped my insides apart. After a while there was laughter and amusing anecdotes flying back and forth across the long tables; all of it blended into a single stream of background noise as I tore my napkin into small pieces and wished for Pop to come back.

12. ALL THE DEVILS ARE HERE

Mono no aware is a phrase that originated in Japan's Heian era (794 – 1185). It translates to "the pathos of things". It is an awareness that everything in life is fleeting - that by their nature, people and experiences are transient: romance will come and go, leaves will change color and fall, youth will submit to old age. Though rooted in sadness for the impermanence of being, it is also intended to promote a celebration of life while it exists. Yoshida Kenkō was a Japanese author and Buddhist monk who expressed this theme perfectly in the 14th century:

"If man were never to fade away like the dews of Adashino, never to vanish like the smoke over Toribeyama, but lingered on forever in this world, how things would lose their power to move us! The most precious thing in life is its uncertainty."

I always visualized the concept of family as a system of floors in a hotel. Each generation represents a floor with the oldest at the top, overlooking everyone else. As a kid, you are essentially standing in the elevator on the ground floor until time begins to pass and you slowly move upward. But there's a catch: while time is passing, additional floors appear beneath you, the topmost floors start to disappear and you realize that you are getting closer to the final parting of the doors, at which point you step out into whatever else the universe has to offer.

In my youth, I always knew that Pop and Gram were on the top floor, followed by their children, and then my parents' generation. Having so many layers above me was comforting, but as the floors peeled away through the natural progression of existence, I felt less and less protected from life.

A month after Pop's funeral, I still hadn't fully processed the finality of everything. Perhaps there was a shred of doubt bouncing around in my head - that Pop was not in the earth, that he would walk through the door or come down the stairs smelling of fresh aftershave. Whatever the case may have been at that time, I was not through grieving because I hadn't started.

One early afternoon, I walked into Clover at Penrose Plaza, a retail chain that no longer exists, but which was as popular as Target or K Mart. The area was always heavily trafficked with shoppers and it was nearly impossible to do anything without others noticing. After browsing for a few moments, the reality of Pop's death suddenly hit me like an oncoming train with no warning. I finally took it all in: he was gone forever and would never come back.

I grabbed the nearest clothing rack and threw it to the ground; I kicked over displays as if I had no concept of my surroundings. I couldn't see the other shoppers staring at me, half-horrified, half-interested like they were driving slowly past a car accident on the highway shoulder. They must have been there, but I couldn't see them. In fact, I don't remember making any noise. I wasn't screaming or punctuating my actions with any kind of verbal outburst; my body was moving on autopilot like a trigger had been activated and I was simply operating on command. I also remember taking a Phillies shirt off its hanger, walking straight into the dressing room, and putting it on under my existing shirt, after which I calmly headed for the store exit.

The cold outside air barely touched my face when I heard someone yelling at me so forcefully that I squinted. *Why does this person have to be so loud?*

"Clover security, come with me," the man said, grabbing my arm and pulling me before I could react.

As I was escorted through the store, I took inventory of the chaos I had left behind. Clothes were strewn across the floor and some poor, overworked employee was trying to put everything in order. I made eye contact with the other shoppers, still unable to grasp what they must have thought as the security guard continued to navigate me towards the back.

We reached the double doors that led to the stock area and made a sharp left into a small, plain-looking room with several black and white monitors broadcasting feeds from different areas of the store. The tag from the inside of the Phillies shirt was irritating the skin on my neck. The guard sat me at a table and placed a tape recorder in front of me, presumably to record my confession to something he already knew I had done. *What's the point of these cameras, then?*

"You want to explain what happened?" he asked, without touching the recorder.

I didn't know what to say. There was no reasoning I could offer that would justify vandalism or theft. Even if I had been honest, there was little chance of being released without a penalty. *The law doesn't care about heartbreak.* Since I wasn't an adult, I tried to calculate the next sequence of events before answering. Just as I had done with my teachers in elementary school, I drew a mental diagram of every possible outcome based on different responses before deciding on one.

The guard nodded his head at the monitors.

"We have cameras all over the store so it's not worth lying."

Who said I was going to lie? Are you from the future? Tell me what tomorrow's winning lottery numbers will be, Biff.

"We know you took the Phillies shirt and you obviously must know we saw you destroying store property," he said.

I looked at the clock on the wall and it was just after 5 p.m. Any other day, I would have been hanging around outside, near home. If I could manage to get out of there within a half-hour, nobody would ever know about my outburst or that I was now sitting in an interrogation room trying to rationalize irrational behavior. I expected to leave after being lectured on what would happen the *next time* I was caught doing something unsavory. Then, I expected that a letter would arrive in the mail a few weeks later recounting the incident and requiring payment to cover the damages. I had a job, and that money would undoubtedly come out of my paycheck. I hated the thought of it, but that would be the extent of their recourse as far as I was concerned.

Instead, the guard stared at me and continued to wait for an explanation.

"I don't know," I said, studying random objects on the walls. The keys hanging on the hook probably belonged to the guard. Maybe they were his house keys or maybe they opened a metal cabinet full of "security guard stuff" like notepads and extra pens for those complex cases that required a lot of jotting and detective work. Maybe he wanted to be a detective and this is the closest he could get; maybe his wife was afraid that he would join the police force and get shot one evening, and that her phone would ring at 2 a.m. with gut-wrenching news from the commissioner. I didn't even know if he was married, but I already had him figured as a would-be Kojak who instead was eking out a living as Clover's version of Batman.

What I hadn't known is that the police had been called before he confronted me by the entrance.

Before he could press me further, two officers entered the room and told me to stand up. The guard grabbed a remote control and rewound the feed on one of the monitors until I saw myself wrecking the store in reverse. He pointed out different things to the officers and followed my image on the screen with his finger. They agreed that it was me. *And the award for brilliance in deduction goes to...*

One of the officers turned me around and handcuffed my hands behind my back before mumbling something into the walkie-talkie on the shoulder of his jacket.

"Am I under arrest?"

"You will be."

"Can I call someone to let them know where I'm going?"

"No, not right now."

Ironically, *I* didn't even know where I was going. The closest police station was the 12th District at 64th & Woodland Avenue. Everyone in Southwest knew that station, not because we had been there, but because Woodland Avenue had become a haven for robberies and the running joke was that it would be faster for the cops to walk to the nearest crime scene than to start their cars and drive there. I guessed that I would be taken to that station and harassed until someone picked me up.

The officer grabbed my bicep and took me through the store. By this time, it was after work hours and the number of shoppers had tripled. Most had not been there when I was having my moment and the mess was no worse than the aftermath of Black Friday, so they were left to speculate on the reason I was in handcuffs. Walking through the metal shelf displays, I heard *Gypsy* by Fleetwood Mac playing over the store speakers; ironically, or maybe as a nod to the world's sometimes-cruel sense of humor, Stevie Nicks had just gotten to the line "...and a memory is all that is left for you now..." as we approached the exit and I left behind the remnants of what can occur when emotional repression collides with agony.

When we got outside, there was a police van with its rear doors open. I stepped up with a push from behind and sat on the metal bench that ran along the inside. Both doors were slammed shut; I thought about the sound of the ambulance doors when Pop had been driven to the hospital a month before.

Because it was winter, it was already dark outside. I had no concept of where the van was going and there were no windows to look through. As I had done on the floor in Patterson during our forced naps, I tried to measure the amount of time on the road and figure out the destination. Every turn was sharply made, which caused me to slide around in the back and slam into the wall a few times. After 15 minutes, I became disoriented and couldn't guess the whereabouts.

When the van slowed to a stop and the officer opened the rear doors, I glanced up the street sign on the corner. They had brought me to the 18th District police station at 55th & Pine for booking. Inside, phones were ringing with abandon. I saw uniforms zigzagging back and forth between desks that were buried under paperwork and almost every surface had an unfinished mug of coffee. To my right was a room with transparent walls; there were three or four people restlessly walking around inside. I was taken to a separate area and fingerprinted. I must have been read my rights and officially arrested, but I don't remember it. After a period of waiting, I was brought to a different officer who told me to pull the laces out of my shoes and take off my belt. When I did, he placed them in a large plastic bag and instructed me to wait in the transparent room with the other people. It was their holding cell.

None of my "cellmates" had their shoelaces or belts either. I sat on a chair against the wall and stared at the drain in the center of the floor. One of the other men was sitting opposite me, and uncharacteristically, I started a conversation.

"Why do we have to give them our laces and belts?"

"So we don't kill ourselves, hang ourselves in here."

I took a quick survey of the room and couldn't find a single thing from which anyone could hang themselves. There wasn't even a door handle on the inside.

"Hang ourselves from what?" I asked.

"Fuck if I know man. Why you here anyway?"

"I...uh, I kicked over some displays at a store and almost stole a t-shirt."

It sounded more frivolous out loud. A few of the other guys snickered in a manner that suggested one of two things: A. It was ridiculous for me to be in a holding cell on such a minor offense or B. I was a lightweight because I hadn't done something more serious. In either case, I was already getting fidgety about leaving. I figured the police would have already alerted my family and I had to think about dealing with them when they arrived.

"What about you?" I asked, trying to stave off the awkwardness.

"Coke," he replied in a long, drawn-out manner that sounded more like "Cooooookkkkkkeeeeeeeee."

"Yeah me too," I heard from another voice in the room. "Coke. That means I'm going back to the center. Shit. I hate the center."

The center. It was so nondescript as if there was only one center in the state of Pennsylvania.

"You're going home tonight," one of them said to me. "Lucky."

Lucky. I didn't feel lucky; I felt disgraced. What would Pop have said to me if he was still alive? This was the last place he would expect me to be. It contradicted every part of my being. I wasn't a troublemaker; were it not for this one slip of reason I would probably be sitting on my front steps as everyone did in my neighborhood, even in cold weather.

I stood up and watched random cops walk past without paying us any attention. Whenever I thought I noticed one of them looking, I mimed putting a telephone up to my face as a way of telling them I wanted to make a call. But almost deliberately, each one of them ignored me, which I could understand from the angle of lawmaker/criminal etiquette but I wasn't *really* a deviant. Surely, they had to know the difference between someone who made a stupid mistake and the usual suspects.

"*Round up the usual suspects...*"

The voice of Claude Rains delivering his famous line in *Casablanca* flashed in my mind, which led me to other memories of watching black and white movies at Pop and Gram's house a decade before. I would have done anything to go back, to rewind my life if that was even theoretically possible, to sink into the worn cushion of their living room sofa with a sleeve of Ritz crackers and all the time in the world.

But, that blip and its place in reality no longer existed anywhere but my heart. I was miles from normal in a glass box trying to plead for the one right I was supposed to have.

Let me make a goddamn phone call!

After a few minutes, I gave up and sat back down. The guys in the room started banging on the wall as a rudimentary way to beatbox and there was suddenly a full-blown concert underway. Because I had grown up in the city and knew most of the lyrics to the songs, I joined in as a way to pass the hours. I *assumed* it would be hours because there was no indication of a process, no steps, no A-Z; I was just waiting without knowing why. I understood the reason for being in jail, but I tried to find an explanation for why anyone would delay processing such a minor offense. *Just get it over with and lighten your own workload! "You cannot escape the responsibility of tomorrow by evading it today."* Lincoln said that, it had to mean something.

At some point, I fell asleep, which is hard to imagine now; but it must have quieted enough for me to doze off and dream, and I was back in the strange, familiar surroundings of my brain's storage cabinet.

"You don't belong here," said an old woman I couldn't identify.

The floor underneath me was gray and airy but also solid. Everywhere I looked, I saw rows of tall cabinets with thousands of drawers that resembled the card catalog system in a library. I felt small and insignificant in their presence because they loomed over me and cast long, black shadows in several directions.

"You don't belong here," the old woman repeated.

She was kind-looking but stern. Her face had deep wrinkles that were almost deliberately carved into her skin and she was dressed in ragged clothing. Without waiting for me to respond, she smirked and turned around to sit in a chair that hadn't been there thirty seconds prior.

"Where am I?" I asked.

"See these cabinets?" she replied.

The moment she finished speaking, some of the drawers began to slide open. They were still too high up for me to see inside, but despite the impossibility, I strained to get a glimpse of their contents.

"Oh, don't bother," said the woman. "You know what's in every drawer here. You know, because you filled each of them yourself."

"I don't remember filling them."

"Well, of course not," she said. "You're reading the wrong book."

"The wrong book?"

"We all have books, several books."

The woman began to run her fingernails over her arm like she was lost in thought while speaking to me.

"Everything you know about yourself and your life..." she continued. "...is in one book. That book is your human memory. When you're remembering the past, you're just flipping the pages back to an earlier chapter you've already read."

"But you said I filled these cabinets that I don't *remember* filling..."

The woman smiled and waited for me to understand what I had just said.

"There is existence outside of *you*," she said. "If you only remember what *you* have done, you miss the point of being in the world."

I looked up at the towering cabinets.

"What are they...really?" I asked.

"The cabinets are the years you have lived. Each one is filled with different thoughts. You created those thoughts."

She stood from her chair and it fell through the mist beneath it.

"This place..." she said. "...is unease. This place is trouble and confusion. Sorrow."

I stared blankly at her.

"You don't belong here."

A thundering sound woke me. When my eyes refocused, I saw two of my cellmates fighting on the opposite side of the room. An officer opened the door and separated them, then escorted one out and into another cell. I looked over and saw the younger of the two men wiping blood from his nose.

Hours later, I was pulled from the holding cell and told to stand beside one of the desks in the office. A digital clock nearby told me it was after 2 a.m. My mother, grandmother, and Rick had arrived to take me home. After the last bit of paperwork was complete, I was led into a new area with a large, presumably bulletproof pane of glass separating us from the people in the waiting room. In the background, I saw Rick wandering back and forth. My mother had a look on her face that combined disappointment, anger, and exhaustion. My grandmother just looked worried.

I don't need this right now. I don't need to be lectured.

A woman sitting at the counter in front of the glass swiveled around and handed me a plastic bag with my belt and shoelaces, then pointed at a door on the left.

"Right through there."

When I entered the waiting area, my welcoming

committee turned and walked out into the parking lot. I followed behind in shame. It felt like Rick had parked the car 200 miles away. We finally reached the parking space and I slid into the backseat next to my grandmother. Nobody said a word.

For 25 minutes I stared through the window at the dark streets. Each time we stopped at a red light, my stomach turned because the tension increased tenfold.

I leaned my head against the glass, closed my eyes, and listened to Pop's voice in my head.

"Look at those big cats," he said, pointing at the cheetahs on his television as their every maneuver was narrated by a British man. "I'll tell ya what, Gary...you'll never see an animal faster than that."

We dropped my grandmother off and went home. Inside the front door, I turned to say something but all I remember was being told that I had to get up for school three hours later. I couldn't argue; I had put myself in that position.

I trudged upstairs and went to bed but didn't sleep. I spent that time trying to imagine where my life was going and where I would ultimately land, now that I was alone again.

13. BOX OF PHOTOS

It took me years after Pop's death to adjust to his absence. The world without him was threatening as if I had been thrown into the deep end of a pool with no way to swim. I never considered him authoritative because he didn't act like someone who enforced rules, but I considered him a father figure in the purest sense.

When I was a kid and needed permission for anything, I asked my mother. My friends always asked their fathers, which confused me since I had never experienced a situation where a male carried any real parental weight. On the contrary, I considered mothers to be supreme rulers in the home, and fathers were merely there for support, but never to supersede the mother's decision or contradict anything she said. I was almost stuck in a reverse-1950s scenario.

Pop didn't undo that way of thinking in me, but what he managed to do was restore my faith in humanity. Everyone in my life, at one point or another, had abandoned me for their own gains. It didn't help if any of it was unintentional; that I felt like I had been moved to the back of the line in more than one sense made me believe that I just didn't matter. My mother leaned too heavily on her assumption that my silence meant happiness and saw no reason to look further, though I'm not sure many parents would have.

The perception that everything is fine makes others feel good. They *want* to believe in the stillness of the water's surface because if they concede that something darker might exist underneath, they either have to address it or ignore its presence - and both require effort.

Rick decided early that I was collateral damage. Whatever his inclinations, he would carry them out regardless of how indifferent he needed to be. His methods of keeping me in line, particularly the staged phone calls and subsequent laughter at my hysterics, gave me severe post-traumatic stress. It sparked a lifelong proclivity for paranoia and distrust, for unrealistic fears that grew into obsessive thinking, for expecting the worse to happen because I thought the universe had randomly selected me for an infinite amount of sadness. I was never more to Rick than a visitor and he made no bones about hiding it. I would like to believe that everything happens for a reason, but some people are just not meant to cross paths. One day, maybe, the reason for those years will reveal itself.

My learned cynicism was kept at bay because Pop was like a dam blocking the torrent of negativity from swallowing me whole, but after he died, I was suddenly thrust back into society without his influence. I reverted to hypervigilance as a protective measure and created problems where they didn't exist because I defined unpredictability as malice. If someone's behavior was inconsistent, it was malignant. The paradox, of course, is that by our nature, we humans are contradictory. Expecting perfect continuity from *anyone* is a recipe for disaster and disappointment. For those with anxiety who look at those changes as a validation of their fear, it's a self-fulfilling prophecy.

In 1998, Gram sold the house for $15,000 and moved in with their daughter, but months before the sale I went down to the basement and looked around.

It's amazing how a person can fill an empty space. It's equally amazing how much emptier that space becomes after they leave. Pop's basement was his laboratory. There were so many projects at different levels of completion that it spoke volumes about his unwillingness to sit idly by while age threatened him. Each plank of wood and pile of bolts represented a part of his life, moments when inspiration struck, good ideas that he wanted to turn into something tangible.

The room was filled with boxes of old decorations, and the storage space beneath the stairs housed lawnmower parts that were presumably scheduled for reassembly at some unknown time. Pop's massive table saw was frozen and still; his cabinets were left open from the last time he had grabbed something in haste and forgotten to close them. A calendar from 1974, yellowed and wrinkled, hung on a rusted carpentry nail bent toward the ceiling.

All of those things, without Pop, were purposeless. For as much as his death had broken me, I never felt more alone than in that moment. I started up the stairs but stopped halfway to sit down, where I put my head into my forearms and cried for an eternity.

My father died on June 10, 2006, at the age of 48 and I didn't find out until August.

"Your father's dead," my mother told me over the phone as if she was talking about the weather.

I remember feeling more stunned than upset. He was always an entity to me, theoretical and *over there*, but still constant. When the reality of his death hit me, a strange void opened and a part of me felt like it was missing. My shock became a determination to find out what happened to him. I started with his death notice.

Gary D. Sweeney of Paulsboro, NJ, [died] suddenly on June 10, 2006. Aged 48 years.

Born in Rome, New York, Gary was a longtime resident of Paulsboro, NJ. He was a carpenter and in his spare time he enjoyed riding his motorcycle, singing, and playing the guitar, organ, and harmonica. He will be sadly missed and will be remembered as a funny, adventurous and loving man.

Beloved Husband of 23 years to Bernice E.

Devoted Father of Joseph, Jonathan, and Matthew.

There was more information, including additional survivors and funeral arrangements, but I stopped reading when I noticed that I had been omitted as a surviving child. His *first* child. The logical part of me tried to reason that I hadn't been in his life and he hadn't been in mine. We were only connected by DNA and a shared name, so maybe it was unfair to expect Bernice to think of me. No matter how rational that seemed, I had one biological father and would never have another. I was entitled to know how and why he died so young, especially if it had been the result of a medical condition.

A few weeks later, the fall weather began to overlap with the heat. The temperature was just warm enough to open the windows and just cool enough to need a light jacket. I sat in my car without the engine running and stared into the empty space between the trees, holding my open flip-phone and debating.

What's the worse she can say? Nothing. She could say nothing.

My heart rate increased a bit. I stared at the digits on the keypad and started punching the number I had found earlier in the day on one of my more vigorous internet searches.

Send.

It rang endlessly, at least in my mind. I don't know how many times it actually rang, but there was an abrupt stop, followed by the jarring cough of a lifetime smoker, a throat clearing, and finally, a *hello*. Bernice's voice was raspy and damaged. I hesitated for a moment. This woman hated me. She hated me because I was a junior. She left my name out of the death notice in an attempt to erase my existence from her husband's past. I prepared myself for the worst and let it go.

"Hello, Bernice," I said cautiously. "This is Gary."

I realized that the last time she had laid eyes on me, I couldn't have been much older than a toddler and probably non-verbal. Now, I was 27 years old and my voice was deeper. Maybe it was just like my father's voice over the phone. She was silent, which I attributed to either awkward discomfort or blatant disbelief. Another couple of seconds passed before I clarified.

"Gary...junior."

Through the amplified noise of her shallow exhales, I could feel the tension. I expected to hear a click. Instead, she replied. "Yes, I remember you."

"How are you?" I asked.

"I'm okay."

I needed a way to transition into my true reason for calling. *What happened to my father?* But I couldn't just turn such a sharp corner without some friendly introductory small talk. The problem was, I didn't know how to be friendly towards her. Even though I had no animosity, there was nothing to say. She was even more of a stranger than my father had been, and with the added knowledge that she resented me for being alive, the last thing I wanted to do was provoke her into hanging up. Oddly, she didn't sound angry; she just sounded defeated from a lifetime of bad decisions, arguments, and one final slap in the face from the universe: widowhood.

"Do you have a few minutes to talk to me?"

"Actually..." she interrupted. "...today is my birthday and I'm a little busy. I have some people over and they're throwing me a party."

"Oh, well, happy birthday!" I replied.

Bernice couldn't have known it, but I had been researching my family tree for a few years and I already knew her birth date, which wasn't even close to that day. It was her way of getting off the phone, perhaps from the confusion of not knowing how to respond. I accepted her lie but asked if I could call her back tomorrow.

"Sure, sure, that would work."

Over the ensuing months, I tried repeatedly to call her but she never answered the phone again. The puzzling circumstances of my father's death continued to monopolize my thoughts. I could not imagine what would cause him to die so abruptly unless it was a freak accident. The only health issue I knew of was his bad back, the origin of which was questionable since he had told my mother it was the result of being kicked by an Army sergeant when he was 17-years-old.

After several dead ends, I was able to contact my

father's brother, James, who was audibly drunk and nearly incoherent over the phone. He knew nothing about the cause of death and didn't seem to care (James died one year later). Endless calls with other relatives ended the same way.

Finally, I contacted two of my half-brothers, Matt and Jon. Matt spent most of the time describing the mountain of VHS tapes in their basement, all of which contained footage of our father. He knew I wanted to see them, so he offered to make copies of each one and mail them to me. All I had to do was send him money through Western Union, which wasn't going to happen for two reasons. First, I didn't want him to have my address; second, he had promised to copy the tapes that evening and mail them the following day. The following day was a Sunday; no postal services were open. I knew immediately he was trying to scam me, a thought confirmed by one of our cousins who knew Matt well enough to warn me of his tactics before our phone call.

Another week passed before I spoke to Jon. He was different than Matt, more reserved, but suspicious of me because Bernice had filled his head with untruths, including the idea that I wanted nothing to do with him. It took a while to convince him otherwise, and when he was comfortable enough to understand that all I needed was answers, he told me he had found our father unresponsive on the bed, cold and in the early stages of rigor mortis. He also casually mentioned that my oldest brother, Joe, immediately began stealing the prescription medicine bottles from our father's nightstand. Jon and I had an amicable conversation, but it became apparent that nobody in my father's life had bothered to obtain his autopsy results. They merely accepted his untimely death and kept going.

The only recourse I had left was to get a death certificate. The state of New Jersey has an exhaustive process for validating the identity of anyone looking for a vital record. A little over two months passed before his death certificate landed in my mailbox; the cause was listed as "adverse effect of drugs" and the manner "accidental."

It was so generic that it created more questions. The term "drugs" alone could have meant too many Advil or it could have meant heroin. Fortunately, the certificate also listed the coroner's name, which I promptly researched until finding contact information. Again, I was asked to prove my identity.

A month later, a large white envelope arrived. The first thing I found was a letter to my attention.

Dear Mr. Sweeney,

Per your request, enclosed is the autopsy report for your father, Gary Sweeney.

If you have any questions regarding this report, please do not hesitate to call this office.

We extend to you and your family, our sympathy in the death of your father.

I pulled the report from the envelope and tore through it, searching for any toxicology results. When I found them, it confirmed the presence of the following:

Urine: Positive for benzodiazepines, oxycodone, acetaminophen, and the respective metabolites.

Blood: Oxycodone, 1.3 mg/L (0.01 - 0.06 mg/L);

oxymorphone, 0.017 mg/L; nordiazepam, 0.55 mg/L; diazepam, 0.13 mg/L (0.2 - 1.6 mg/L); acetaminophen, 8.0 mg/L.

Fentanyl Screen: Negative in urine and blood.

Everything in his system appeared to be a prescription medication. His longstanding back problems, from what I knew, had become so bad that he was eventually dependent on a morphine pump. My uneducated guess was that the drugs in his system were for pain management and that the frequency with which he took them raised his tolerance until he needed an inordinate amount to feel normal. But that was an amateur hypothesis at best; I wasn't sure if it was the amount of medication he took, the combination of those specific medications, or both.

After some digging, I found information that suggested a high level of danger when Opiates and Benzodiazepines are mixed. Specifically, the combination of the two depresses a person's breathing to the point of nonresponsiveness, which will eventually kill them if there is no medical intervention.

Information provided by American Addiction Centers stated:

"According to the American Society of Addiction Medicine, in 2014, there were 18,893 prescription painkiller-related overdose deaths in the US. Between 1999 and 2006, there was a 250 percent increase in fatal overdoses in the United States due to opioid painkillers; more than half of those overdoses were due to a combination of opioid painkillers and another medication, most typically benzodiazepines. For people hospitalized due to a benzodiazepine overdose between 1998 and 2008, 95 percent of the time, benzodiazepines were combined with another drug; in 54.2 percent of those cases, opiate drugs (heroin or prescription painkillers) were the other drug in the combination.

"This combination appears to be especially dangerous because benzodiazepines enhance the "high" from opioid painkillers. When people become addicted to opioid painkillers like Vicodin or oxycodone, they can develop a tolerance over time so they do not experience the same effect; however, when these individuals add benzodiazepines to the mix, they can return to the same euphoric feeling they had the first time they abused opioids.

"One of the two biggest problems with mixing opioid painkillers like Vicodin or oxycodone with benzodiazepines like Xanax or Valium is the issue of oversedation. This is the inability to wake up or respond to stimuli, which can put individuals at risk of falling if they are standing up, or causing a serious car accident if they are driving. People could also slip into a coma.

"Additionally, both opioid painkillers and benzodiazepines can change breathing patterns — specifically, they can both depress breathing. This condition leads to a lack of oxygen to the brain, eventually shutting down vital organ systems, leading to brain damage and even death."

When my half-brother Jon told me that he had found our father cold and unresponsive on the bed, it confirmed much of what I had read in the autopsy report. Now, I was the only person (aside from the professionals) who knew the exact reason for my father's death. I don't believe Bernice even knew.

The moment I had the answer, I began wondering how much I may have been like my father. Perhaps my anxiety and excessive thinking were genetic, and maybe the only difference between me and my father was that I had someone like Pop to save me from self-destruction. He had nobody. My father was raised in an abusive household with constant fighting and screaming. Maybe he had a low tolerance for noises like I had, maybe he was overloaded with stimuli and lashed out at others because he couldn't adapt and there was no one he could turn to for help.

It was possible. There certainly wasn't anyone else in my family who acted like me. More than anything, I finally wanted to sit and talk with him as an adult, to figure things out. We may not have gotten along, or we may have connected on a hundred levels. But now that I had the desire, I no longer had the chance. It's one of the great regrets of my life that we never cleared the air.

In 2017, I drove to 3900 Wissahickon Avenue to visit the hollowed remains of Midvale. Of the numerous buildings that once dominated the landscape, only two were left standing on the backlot of what had become a SEPTA bus depot. My wife and I stepped cautiously into the first warehouse. It was eerily silent with dust particles raining down between piercing shafts of afternoon light. Random pieces of broken metal peppered the wet cement floor; torn plastic swayed in the soft breeze coming through the tall windows. I closed my eyes and heard the roar of the machines; I listened to the men talking loudly to one another; I imagined the relief at quitting time when everyone removed their hats and walked away. Then I opened my eyes and the room was empty again.

All that was left were ghosts.

In some way, I was staring Midvale's death in the face. I was able to see how large it had been, how completely immovable and safe it would have appeared to its workers. And, I was able to feel the horror of its rapid descent, like another Titanic or Hindenburg disappearing into nothingness. I then realized that Pop had been my personal Midvale, imperishable and made of steel, until suddenly he wasn't there.

14. OTHER DAYS

In his poem *A Servant of Servants*, Robert Frost wrote:
Len says one steady pull more ought to do it.
He says the best way out is always through.
Those lines became my anchor for survival on numerous occasions. *The best way out is always through*. None of us get away from life unscathed. We're all destined to encounter hardships, loss, and some level of trauma that either destroys us, embitters us, or pushes us into a corner until we have no choice but to fight back. Some experience more pain than others and it can seem unfair when we measure ourselves against the rest of the population as though we're owed a certain amount of happiness. But regardless of how much pain we're dealt, or how many times we feel like we've reached the end of our ability to cope, the fact remains: the best way out is always through. We can't avoid life or find shortcuts to minimize its impact; we have to let the swords cut us to pieces, bleed, and move forward.

It's easy to go back through the early years of my life

and feel sadness. But, I don't. I feel the opposite. There's a level of gratitude that remains because I look at where I came from and realize that so many people have dealt with anxiety and depression without an outlet. I can't fathom how anyone could swerve through existence and not let their demons run free once in a while, even though, as in my case, they may run across the page and seep back into your pores. I was able to step back and examine my life, knowing the consternation that plagued me since childhood would never fully go away. I learned to deal with it more effectively, and it rarely suffocates me anymore, but it will always hide somewhere with vitriolic intent, waiting for the right time to sneak past my defenses. I suppose some of us are just wired that way.

There is a popular therapeutic tactic where someone writes their regrets on small pieces of paper and then burns them. The rising smoke is supposed to signify the release of those burdens to a higher power, or even to the universe. Once the ashes blow away, those problems are gone forever. I understand the beauty of the symbolism and why it works. For me, this book has been its own fire.

I'm also grateful because I had Pop. My introversion extended all the way to my own family, but for some reason, I was always myself around him. He's probably the only person who ever really knew me. And still, there are moments I can recall where I wish I had been more open. I know that no matter how odd or quirky I may have seemed to other people my age, Pop would have accepted me - and encouraged me to continue being myself.

For as mythical as he appeared to be, I realize that Pop was simply a kind person at a time when I needed kindness. He was like that with everyone to some degree, but we had a bond that surpassed the normal grandparent/grandchild relationship. He never tried to control me or belittle my worth because I was a kid in a world of adults.

The most important thing I have taken from the part of my life he occupied is this: you can make an immeasurable difference to somebody, to their path and their future, to their ability to see a way out, by just being present.

That's what he was, present.

Whenever I see a woman standing by the fruit in a grocery store, I smile to myself. When I'm surrounded by nature, I think of how much he would have loved it. I can still see him unpacking his folding chair and placing it under a tree to sit, and just exist, as part of creation.

Though I loved Gram just as much, I had no shortage of women in my family. I could identify with any woman based solely on my exposure to them and their ways of viewing the world. But as a young boy, what I needed most was a dad.

I spent a lot of time wondering if I hadn't meant enough to my father for him to bother visiting me. Even when I learned that Bernice forbade him to see me, it did little to stop the circling questions about how important I was to him, or why he didn't try harder or fight against his wife's objections. When other boys played catch with their fathers, I stared at my baseball glove sitting unused in the corner of the room and imagined my three half-brothers tossing the ball around.

It felt almost impossible to capture the essence of just *knowing* someone because everything is nuance. A person's totality is found in subtleties, tones, layers, and shades. It comes through in how they interact and respond, in their opinions and predictability. When we recognize those things and can easily define them as the representation of another human being, we've established a connection, perhaps one only knowable to ourselves. Sending that information out into the world and hoping it resonates is an arduous task. But I had to try. For as hard as this book was at times, I'm glad I stuck with it. My daughter now has a tangible record of someone who mattered greatly to me. If no one else in the world reads this, I'm grateful to have put this timeline together for her.

One of my greatest fears is the idea that history can disappear with a single person. If we don't tell our stories, they will eventually drift into the ages and burn out. The only way we'll live forever is if people love us enough to keep us alive. It's not enough to simply remember; we need to write, record and preserve.

Pop turned 64 just after I was born, but it was an old 64. It was a 64 with years of hard labor stacked underneath, of aching bones and shooting pains, of high blood pressure and quietly declining health. By the time I was old enough to envy my friends and their attentive fathers, Pop was over 70 and in no condition to undertake any kind of physical activity.

Still, I have memories that I wouldn't trade for a million more lifetimes. I have the sound of his laugh and the look on his face when he hauled me out of Patterson early because he knew I didn't want to be there; I have the leathery smell of his Skylark's dashboard in the summer when we drove with the windows down; I have the library of random facts he carved into my mind; I have his love of animals; I have his good heart.

As of this writing, he's been gone 25 years.

I still miss him every day.

POSTFACE

Gram used to brag that she would be the first one of her siblings to live to 90. Most of her older brothers and sisters died in their 70s and she was looking forward to the milestone. She ended up passing away on August 13, 2007, the day before her 90th birthday. In her later years, Gram talked very little about Pop. Every so often, I would catch her reminiscing about old times or humming some pre-war melody. But that was the extent of it.

After her passing, I inherited the remaining decorative items from their home and the stacks of papers she had saved for decades. Among a pile of documents was the deed to their house (purchased for $2,450 in 1945, approximately $36,000 in today's money). Although it feels strange to admit, there is something calming about having posthumous "ownership" of that home, despite the fact that someone else is currently living there and the inside is unlikely to match the layout I remember. But, in some way, keeping that paper folded safely in a box and tucked away, has frozen that small hiding place of mine in perpetuity.

The papers Gram had saved also included the deed to Billy's still-unmarked grave in Fernwood Cemetery. It cost a total of $3,695 to have Billy prepared for burial and then interred after a small church service that almost nobody attended (aside from Pop and Gram). Now that I understand how sparse their financial situation had been at that time, Billy's anonymous grave makes total sense. Having researched the tragic history of Pennhurst and realizing that, aside from Pop's visits, Billy lived as a disposable member of society, I plan to mark his grave in the near future as a way to remember him.

On occasion, I still think about my father. I went through a period of mourning in my mid-30s where I felt a great sense of loss. I missed my father even though he was never a significant figure in my life. I saw him looking back at me when I stood before a mirror; I heard his laugh in my own. I was fortunate to connect with some first cousins on my father's side who shared their memories of him — some funny, some not worth bragging about.

The only possession of my father's that I own is a ring given to him by my mother for Christmas 1977, just a few weeks after they began dating. At that point, she hadn't known him well enough and expected a thoughtful gift in return. She later discovered that he had stolen a bunch of perfume from the drugstore as his gift to her. Throughout the rest of their relationship, she only bought him chocolate or personalized items to ensure he wouldn't sell them. Just before he left for good, she managed to grab the ring back.

My middle brother, Jonathan, died in 2013 at the age of 27. He had battled health issues and addiction his entire life. At the time of his death, he had already suffered two strokes, had open heart surgery, and numerous ruptured discs in his back. He left behind four children. Shortly after he died, I was in touch with his girlfriend, who routinely dropped by to visit with Bernice so she could see two of her grandchildren. Jon's girlfriend informed me that Bernice had my father's ashes sitting on a mantle, surrounded by pictures of him smiling and lifting his beer toward the photographer. Some part of me wishes that I had his ashes instead, and that I could bury them in a peaceful setting in a final act of closure – as a way of saying, "I will take care of you, even though you could not take care of me."

During the editing process, I had several discussions with family members about the contents of this book. Perhaps the most enlightening thing to come from those discussions was the revelation that my anxiety did not begin with me. My mother also suffers from anxiety but did not understand that her symptoms were considered such. Gram would casually mention having a "nervous stomach" and Pop spoke randomly about feelings that could easily define Generalized Anxiety Disorder. Of course, he believed that eating oatmeal regularly cured just about everything.

When I was a kid, I always use to tell myself that things would change one day, that there would be other days when I wouldn't feel cloistered, when the world would illuminate and throw open the shutters to fill me with hope. Now that I am a father, I am finding redemption in my daughter. In her, I have the opportunity to be present, as Pop was for me. I can praise her for her strengths and talents; I can be there when she's afraid or confused. If I notice any behaviors resembling the ones I had as a child, she will have the benefit of knowing that I understand. I can remind her that no matter how dark the world can be, there is always a bit of light, if you know where to find it.

Photographs

Pop at Midvale.

Midvale to close forging plant; 600 to lose jobs

By Jane Shoemaker
Inquirer Business Writer

Midvale-Heppenstall Co. announced yesterday that it would shut its forging operation in Philadelphia's Nicetown section by March 31, putting 600 persons out of work.

The company said it could no longer afford to buy the high-priced oil needed to run the plant's machinery and has been unable to borrow enough money to buy new equipment that uses less fuel.

Carl E. Anderson, chief executive of both Midvale-Heppenstall and its parent, Pittsburgh-based Heppenstall Co., said that fuel costs tripled in 1975 alone.

At the same time, he said, the plant's bookings have dwindled. Most of Midvale-Heppenstall's customers are utilities, and many of them have canceled or postponed construction projects because of the weak economy.

Anderson estimated that $16 million of expected new orders were not booked last year and that another $20 million of old orders had been canceled.

The firm's financial situation was damaged further by a 10-week strike last summer that idled the Nicetown plant, he said.

Anderson said that he had been looking for more than a year for a buyer of Midvale-Heppenstall's Nicetown operation.

"We just can't find one," he said in a telephone interview from Pittsburgh. "I guess every company has its own problems in raising money for things they want to do. They don't want to take this on knowing that it needs another $18 million to $20 million for new equipment."

The first mention of Midvale's closing.
The Philadelphia Inquirer - January 29, 1976

The "Over the Hill Gang." Gram is standing and smiling. Pop is standing at top right. Seated at bottom left are my paternal grandparents, Earl & Bernadette Sweeney.

Left: My father holding me.

Bottom: My father in Pop & Gram's kitchen.

Top: My mother and me.

Left: With my mother and father at Pop & Gram's house.

Pop and me on his back porch.

With Pop & Gram at my 2nd birthday party.

Fun and
french fries at
Pop & Gram's
kitchen table.

Waiting with Pop to see Mayor Frank Rizzo.

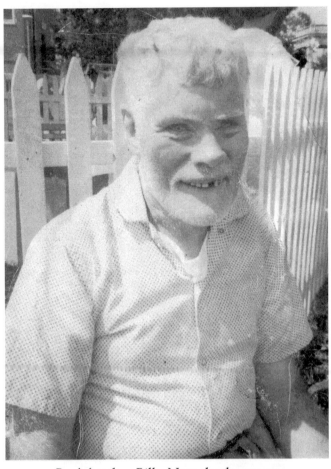
Pop's brother, Billy. Note the damage to
his left eye from Pennhurst.

Me with Rick (holding his trademark umbrella).

With Pop & Gram around the time I started first grade.

The last fishing trip we ever took.
Perkiomen Falls - Schwenksville, Pennsylvania.
July 15, 1991

Pop & Gram the way I remember them best.

Pop standing in front of the cake and holding his mandolin at his 80th birthday party.

Mantua, New Jersey

March 26, 1995

The remains of Midvale in 2017.

My favorite vintage photos of Pop & Gram.

Made in the USA
Middletown, DE
23 February 2022